D0321815

# WYNNERE AND WASTOURE

EARLY ENGLISH TEXT SOCIETY

No. 297

1990

# WYNNERE AND WASTOURE

EDITED BY

STEPHANIE TRIGG

*Published for*
THE EARLY ENGLISH TEXT SOCIETY
*by the*
OXFORD UNIVERSITY PRESS
1990

Oxford University Press, Walton Street, Oxford OX2 6DP
Oxford New York Toronto
Delhi Bombay Calcutta Madras Karachi
Petaling Jaya Singapore Hong Kong Tokyo
Nairobi Dar es Salaam Cape Town
Melbourne Auckland
Associated companies in Beirut Berlin Ibadan Nicosia

Oxford is a trade mark of Oxford University Press

British Library Cataloguing in Publication Data
Wynnere and Wastoure.—(Original series/Early English
Text Society; no. 297).
I. Trigg, Stephanie    II. Series
821'.1
ISBN 0–19–722299–4

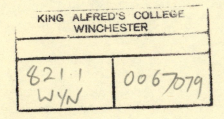

Set by Joshua Associates Limited, Oxford
Printed in Great Britain
by Richard Clay (The Chaucer Press) Ltd.,
Bungay, Suffolk

*For my family—*
*Una, Wesley, Jocelyn, and Fiona*

# PREFACE

It is a pleasure to acknowledge the assistance and support of the many colleagues and friends who have helped me at different stages in my work on this text, especially Mary Dove, Gregory Kratzmann, and Jenna Mead. In particular, I would like to record my thanks to George Russell for his patient and generous advice and encouragement. Kevin Hart discussed many aspects of the work with me, and read the manuscript with scrupulous attention to detail: my greatest debt is to him. I am grateful to the British Library for permission to reproduce a page of BL Additional MS 31042 as the frontispiece.

# CONTENTS

# PLATE

# ABBREVIATIONS

| | |
|---|---|
| AN&Q | American Notes and Queries |
| Archiv | Archiv für das Studium der Neueren Sprachen und Literaturen |
| EETS, ES, SS | Early English Text Society, Extra Series, Supplementary Series |
| ELH | ELH, A Journal of English Literary History |
| ES | English Studies |
| ESt | Englische Studien |
| LeedsSE | Leeds Studies in English |
| MÆ | Medium Ævum |
| MLN | Modern Language Notes |
| MLQ | Modern Language Quarterly |
| MLR | Modern Language Review |
| MP | Modern Philology |
| N&Q | Notes and Queries |
| NM | Neuphilologische Mitteilungen |
| PBSA | Papers of the Bibliographical Society of America |
| RES | Review of English Studies |
| SAC | Studies in the Age of Chaucer |
| SB | Studies in Bibliography |
| SMC | Studies in Medieval Culture |

# INTRODUCTION

## THE MANUSCRIPT

The single text of *Wynnere and Wastoure* is found in British Library Additional MS 31042, the smaller of two miscellanies compiled by Robert Thornton in the fifteenth century. The London manuscript was written after the 1420s or 1430s, when some of the poems by Lydgate or in imitation of his style must have been written, and before Thornton's death *c.* 1468.[1] Recent research on Thornton suggests he was working concurrently on this and his other compilation, Lincoln Cathedral MS 91, in the early years of the second half of the fifteenth century.[2]

Several religious histories and verse romances are grouped together at the beginning of the miscellany, including imperfect versions or fragments of the *Cursor Mundi*, *The Northern Passion*, *The Sege of Jerusalem*, and *The Sege of Melayne*.[3] Texts of *Richard the Lionheart* and *The Childhode of Jesus Criste* appear towards the end of the manuscript, which also includes several poems by Lydgate, a number of carols, and other devotional or ethical poems, including *A Louely Song of Wysdome*, 'Waste makes a kyngdome in nede', and an incomplete paraphrase of Psalm 51, 'God þou haue mercy of me', in rhyming alliterative stanzas. Alliterative poetry is well represented in the collection; also featured are *The Quatrefoil of Love* and the only complete text of *The Parlement of the Thre Ages*, preceding *Wynnere and Wastoure* at the end of the manuscript. With the exception of three Latin proverbs, all the items are in English.

The manuscript itself is a quarto volume, comprising 181 paper leaves of rather coarse quality and four vellum fly-leaves from a fifteenth-century Breviary. The first and last paper leaves are discoloured and torn and it seems that the Breviary leaves were attached

---

[1] See K. M. Stern, 'The London "Thornton" Miscellany: A New Description of BM Addit. MS. 31042', *Scriptorium*, xxx (1976), 26–37, 201–18, p. 211. H. N. MacCracken, 'Lydgatiana', *Archiv*, cxxix (1912), p. 50, considers that the *Verses on the Kings of Cologne*, for example, are an imitation of Lydgate's *Legend of St Edmund*, written in 1433.

[2] George R. Keiser, 'Lincoln Cathedral Library MS. 91: Life and Milieu of the Scribe', *SB* xxxii (1979), 158–79, 162; and Ralph Hanna III, 'The Growth of Robert Thornton's Books', *SB* xl (1987), 51–61.

[3] A complete catalogue of the manuscript's contents is found in Stern, pp. 214–18.

to the manuscript at a much later date. The leaves have been unevenly
trimmed and vary in size from 270–4 mm. in height by 196–206 mm. in
width, while the height of the written space averages 214 mm. With the
exception of ff. 101–2, containing the psalm paraphrase, each leaf is
ruled for single or double columns in brown ink or drypoint, but
pricking is not always evident. A frame of red ink encloses the first half
of the text of *Richard the Lionheart*.

Prior to 1972 the manuscript was bound too tightly to allow any
examination of the sewing, and when it was re-bound and guarded,
the sewing holes were lost, and no record of its composition was taken.
The manuscript is incomplete at beginning and end, moreover, and at
least eight leaves are missing from other parts of the manuscript. With
the exception of the two stubs after f. 110, all the leaves were num-
bered 1–183 in pencil on the top right-hand corner of the leaf in 1880
when the manuscript was bound by the British Museum. There is a
fainter sequence on the lower left-hand corner of the recto side of each
leaf, which counts 1–181 by ignoring the first two fly-leaves; however,
the upper, more legible sequence, has been used by Stern and all other
editors of the manuscript.

Any collation of the manuscript must now depend on the analysis of
watermarks and the scribe's arrangement of texts into different groups
and sequences according to subject-matter. Robert Thornton tended
to work with large folio gatherings, and both manuscripts seem to have
been compiled in separate quires, or at least, booklets of one or more
quires. It seems likely that the Lincoln and the London manuscripts
were assembled from a common stock of materials, and the scribe may
well have been compiling several booklets or fascicles at a time,
grouping his material according to its subject matter. Thornton can be
described as a careful amateur, copying texts not on commission or
under supervision, but for his own use and that of his family.[1]

The most persuasive collations are those which take both watermark evidence and the disposition of texts into account, and Ralph
Hanna III divides the London manuscript into eleven quires.[2] He

---

[1] Keiser (1979); and 'More Light on the Life and Milieu of Robert Thornton', *SB*
xxxvi (1983), 111–19.

[2] Stern offered a conjectural collation of several quires in her description, but this
was superseded by Sarah M. Horrall, 'The London Thornton Manuscript: A New Collation', *Manuscripta*, xxiii (1979), 99–103, and 'The Watermarks on the Thornton Manuscripts', *N&Q* n.s. xvii (1980), 385–6. Hanna accepts much of Horrall's work, but is more
willing to use watermark evidence to reconstruct the quires, in 'The London Thornton
Manuscript: A Corrected Collation', *SB* xxxvii (1984), 122–30; and 'The Growth of
Robert Thornton's Books'.

argues that the scribe probably started with gatherings of eight or nine sheets, supplementing these from the centre, if necessary. Hanna also divides these quires into the booklets in which Thornton probably copied and assembled the miscellany.

Booklet I: (*Cursor Mundi* excerpts) $1^7$ ff. 3–8, $2^{24}$ ff. 9–32;
Booklet IIa: (*The Northern Passion*, romances) $3^{22}$ (−22) ff. 33–53, $4^{20}$ ff. 54–73, $5^{26}$ (−5, −8, −26) ff. 74–96;
Booklet IIb: (religious verse) $6^7$ ff. 97–102, $7^{18}$ (−1, −10, −11) ff. 103–17, $8^{6+1}$ (+7) ff. 118–24;
Booklet III: (*Richard the Lionheart*, *The Childhode of Jesus Criste*) $9^{22+1}$ (−20, −21, −22, +23) ff. 125–44; $10^{24}$ ff. 145–68; and
Booklet IV: (*The Parlement of the Thre Ages*; *Wynnere and Wastoure*) $11^{18}$ (−14, −15, −16, −17, −18, most cancels) ff. 169–81.

This last booklet concerns us most: it consists of four full sheets, three half-sheets with watermark and two half-sheets without mark. The presence of the two alliterative debate poems in the one booklet suggests that they were copied from the same source, and Hanna construes this as the putative 'Doncaster exemplar' which contained Thornton's texts for a number of other works, mostly romances, copied in both manuscripts.[1] Hanna concedes that much of this work is highly speculative and hypothetical, though all the evidence does point to considerable enthusiasm, effort, and care on Thornton's part. The last leaf of the incomplete *Wynnere and Wastoure* is copied in two columns, however, and this might imply a degree of haste or misjudgement.

Thornton's script is a traditional anglicana, usually small and well-formed but variable in size. Dismissing earlier claims that this variation indicated the work of several scribes, K. Hodder (Stern) finds a different hand of approximately the same date only in the carol-fragments on f. $94^v$.[2] Punctuation is infrequent, confined to a mark [:] which might indicate a breathing-space, though it is sometimes used with another mark [:/] to signify a rhythmic break where two lines of verse have been copied as one. Neither of these symbols is used in the text of *Wynnere and Wastoure*. Most texts feature coloured capitals which extend down for between two and five lines, in red, green, or

[1] Hanna (1987), p. 55, draws on the earlier linguistic analysis of Thornton's texts by A. McIntosh, 'The Textual Transmission of the Alliterative *Morte Arthure*', in *English and Medieval Studies Presented to J. R. R. Tolkien* (London, 1962), pp. 231–40.

[2] K. Hodder (Stern), 'Two Unpublished Middle English Carol-Fragments', *Archiv*, ccv (1969), 378–83.

blue ink, while a smaller form of the capital in brown ink is often still visible in the margin as a guide to the rubricator. Only *The Northern Passion* is illustrated with several small ink drawings.

The manuscript was bought by the British Museum on 12 July 1879 from John Pearson, a London bookseller. It was foliated, bound, and examined in February 1880, then re-bound, repaired, and guarded in January 1972.

## THE SCRIBE

The scribe has signed his manuscript twice, on ff. 50$^r$ and 66$^r$, after *The Northern Passion* and *The Sege of Jerusalem*. There is little doubt now that the Robert Thornton who copied this manuscript and Lincoln Cathedral Library MS 91 was Robert Thornton, lord of East Newton in Ryedale, Yorkshire.[1] George Keiser's research into surviving legal records has built up a comparatively detailed picture of the scribe's social milieu and his role in public life, as someone who served as a tax collector and on a number of occasions, as a witness and executor. Thornton reached his majority in 1418 on the death of his father and by virtue of his considerable land-holdings, he must have attained 'some moderate prestige and influence' and 'a respectable degree of prosperity' before his death *c.* 1468.[2] Keiser proposes a number of avenues through which Thornton may have obtained access to his exemplars. The name Robert Thornton is found in wills, quitclaim deeds, and other documents linked with the larger Yorkshire manors of Northolm and Great Edston, and Keiser raises the possibility that the scribe might have come into contact with some of the wealthy and powerful men associated with these manors, at least two of whom had libraries of their own: John Kempe, Archbishop of York, and Robert Stillyngton, bishop of Bath and Wells. Thornton is also named in the public records with a number of lesser clerics and landowners whose wills mention books or manuscripts closely linked to items copied by Thornton in both his collections.[3] For example, the scribe served as an executor to Sir Richard Pikeryng of Oswaldkirk, whose descend-

---

[1] For a summary of scholarship, see the facsimile of *The Thornton Manuscript*, with introductions by A. E. B. Owen and D. S. Brewer (London, 1975, rev. 1977). See also Stern, pp. 204–5.

[2] Keiser (1979), pp. 158–79, 162. Thornton was previously thought to have died before 1465, but Keiser notes a charter dated 1468 in the Close Rolls which is witnessed by a Robert Thornton whom he identifies as the scribe.

[3] Keiser (1979), pp. 165–74.

ants in the sixteenth century owned a text of the *Liber de diversis medicinis* closely related to the text in the Lincoln manuscript. In addition, Sir Richard's sister, Joan, became a nun at the priory of St Mary at Nun Monkton, which owned a number of books in the mid-fifteenth century, and although there are no direct links between Thornton's texts and those books mentioned in bequests to the priory, Keiser proposes that the library of St Mary's is another likely source for the scribe's exemplars.[1]

Thornton's two manuscripts display a curious mixture of professional features with a somewhat casual or at least inconsistent approach and it seems likely that in matters of formatting and presentation he was influenced to some degree by his exemplars. As we have seen, parts of each compilation seem to follow an ordered sequence, though the London manuscript also shows signs of compression. Short pieces and tags often appear at the end of quires, while the last lines of a longer work are sometimes squeezed on to the last side of a gathering. From the greater care taken in copying and decorating the first two items (the *Cursor Mundi* fragments and *The Northern Passion*), Stern argues that Thornton was a 'pious copyist' who gave greater prominence to religious poems; but problems of classification inevitably arise: *The Sege of Jerusalem* is described as a 'romance' when it is copied with less care after *Cursor Mundi* and the *Passion*, but 'part of a series of poems on sacred history' when it boasts the only decorated initial capital.[2]

Guddat-Figge suggests that the manuscript was commissioned for a wealthy family, but can offer no supporting evidence for this claim.[3] On the contrary, all the evidence supports the thesis that Thornton was working for himself and his family, and the contents of both collections are a valuable indication of the fifteenth-century middle class interest in vernacular romance and in ethical and devotional literature. The Lincoln manuscript remained in the Thornton family for several generations, and the names of several family members were recorded on its pages before it found its way to the Cathedral in the late seventeenth-century.[4] There are marks of other ownership on the London manuscript though, which suggest it passed out of the family

[1] Keiser (1983), pp. 114–19.
[2] Stern, p. 33.
[3] G. Guddat-Figge, *Catalogue of Manuscripts Containing Middle English Romances* (Munich, 1976), p. 161.
[4] G. R. Keiser, 'The Nineteenth-Century Discovery of the Thornton Manuscript (Lincoln Cathedral Library MS. 91)', *PBSA* lxxvii (1983), 167–90.

in the sixteenth century, and came into the hands of John Nettleton of Hutton Cranswick in the East Riding of Yorkshire, who is known to have owned other manuscripts. Nothing is known of its subsequent history until it reappeared in London in 1879.

Thornton's text of *Wynnere and Wastoure* appears on ff. 176ᵛ–181ᵛ, and is written in generously spaced single columns until f. 181 (the last leaf of the manuscript) which is ruled recto and verso in double columns. There are many more abbreviations and contractions used on the last leaf (lines 353–503), where the hand is generally smaller and more cramped. While Thornton is usually careful to check his exemplar, and ready to make corrections, none appears on this last leaf, suggesting he may also have been pressed for time. Interestingly, in these last four columns he has not been so concerned to preserve the dialectal forms of his exemplar, and of the more distinctive Northern forms in the poem the majority appears in this last third of the text. Moreover, on this last leaf, the letter *ȝ* makes its sole appearance as the palatal spirant in *nyȝte*, line 478, and then once as the final voiced sibilant in *hasteleteȝ*, at line 492. These examples presumably reflect the scribe's usage, although he has by no means superimposed a heavy layer of Northernisms on his exemplar, and this seems to be characteristic of his work as a whole.[1]

## DATE AND PROVENANCE

*Language*

The dialect of *Wynnere and Wastoure* is almost identical to that of *The Parlement of the Thre Ages*, and is examined in some detail by M. Y. Offord in her edition of that poem.[2] It is generally agreed that these two poems share the same mixture of dialectal features, although early arguments for common authorship are now regarded as inconclusive.[3] The account that follows makes no claims to be comprehensive and concentrates on those linguistic features of the poem which seem to indicate its original dialect.

We have only two pieces of non-linguistic evidence to help us

---

[1] See McIntosh, p. 232; and Mary Hamel, 'Scribal Self-Corrections in the Thornton *Morte Arthure*', *SB* xxxvi (1983), p. 135.

[2] *The Parlement of the Thre Ages*, ed. M. Y. Offord, EETS 246 (1959), pp. xvii–xxvi. See also R. S. Rainbow, 'A Linguistic Study of *Wynnere and Wastoure* and *The Parlement of the Thre Ages*' (Ph.D. diss., Chicago, 1960).

[3] Offord summarizes the debate, pp. xxxiv–xxxvi.

determine the original provenance of *Wynnere and Wastoure*: the certain location of Robert Thornton in the North Riding of Yorkshire in the middle of the fifteenth century and the narrator's two hints of a Western provenance at line 7, *Dare neuer no westren wy . . .* and at line 32, *Als I went in the weste. . . .* These lines are part of the poet's framing fiction, though, and should be read against his obvious knowledge of the city of London and concern with international politics.

Furthermore, the degree of textual corruption in the poem bears witness to several stages of copying between the poet's original composition and our only surviving copy, while at this comparatively late date for a manuscript of Middle English, we cannot always be sure whether seemingly Southern or South-East Midlands forms indicate the hand of a Southern copyist or the spread of London forms. Thornton seems fairly tolerant of non-Northern forms, but his text of *Wynnere and Wastoure* nevertheless exhibits a variety of dialectal features.

We can exclude the possibility of an extreme Southern origin, for the only distinctive Southern forms are several examples of *-eth* and *-ith* in 3 sg. pr. indic. (*brynneth*, *draweth*, *lyketh*, *biddith*, *ledith*, &c.), and one in 3 pl. (*owthe*, 329), and these are probably London forms accepted by the poet.

There are more Northern forms, but only to a degree commensurate with our expectations of a Midlands or North Midlands text copied by a Yorkshire scribe.

§1 OE *ā*, ON *á* > *a* in *clade*, *mare*, *twa*, etc., although rounding to *o* is more common.

§2 OE *y̆* appears most commonly as *i* or *y*, in *fill*, *girdels*, *rigge*, *dyn*, *pryde*, *ryme*, etc., a feature shared with East Midlands dialects.

§3 OE *o* > *u* in *gude*, *lukis*, and *luke*, but *o* normally remains without fronting, as in *gode*, *lokes*, *blode*, *come*, *flode*, etc.

§4 The raising of *e* to *i* after *r* in *ristyth* and *priste* might represent a Northern development but is also found in the East and South-East Midlands.[1]

§5 OE *sc* is found in unstressed syllables as *s* in *sall* (once only) and *Ynglysse*. These are probably scribal forms: note also Thornton's correction of *sh* to *s* in *sall*, line 179.

§6 The feminine pronoun throughout is *scho*.

§7 The plural pronominal forms are *þay*, *they*, *þaire*, *thayre*, *þam*,

---

[1] J. and E. M. Wright, *An Elementary Middle English Grammar* (2nd edn., Oxford, 1928), §127; K. Luick, *Historische Grammatik der englischen Sprache* (Leipzig, 1914–40), §379.

and *thaym*. The only exceptions are *hire* and reconstructed *h[em]* (MS *hir*) at lines 13, 15.

§8 3 sg. pr. indic. most commonly takes *-es*, sometimes *-is*, *-ys*, e.g. *askes*, *begynnes*, *comes*, *dwellys*, *fightis*.

§9 Occasionally *-es* is found in pl. pr. indic., e.g. *ʒemes*, *knowes*.

§10 Imper. pl. ends in *-es* in *blynnes* and possibly *welcomes* (see note to line 212).

§11 The inflectional *-ande* in pr. ptc. *daderande*, *neghande*, etc. is probably Northern rather than extreme East or West Midlands.

§12 The Northern indication of vowel quantity in *titmoyses* is almost certainly scribal.

The predominant cast of the language can best be loosely described as North Midlands. Perhaps surprisingly, there are few distinctive West Midlands forms:

§13 OE *ў > u* in *blussche*, *full*.

§14 OE *a/o* before a nasal consonant *> o* in *bonke*, *plontes*, but forms with *a* predominate. Luick describes this development as a feature of the West Midlands, and perhaps an area southwards, but Moore, Meech, and Whitehall, and also Kristensson, find examples in the West Riding of Yorkshire.[1]

§15 The pronominal forms *hire*, gen. pl. and *h[em]*, acc. pl. at lines 13 and 15 are evidence of Western, or perhaps Southern forms in Thornton's exemplar (see Commentary).

These forms must be weighed against the non-Western features such as:

§16 Forms with *i, y* for OE *ў* (§2) and even with *e* in *mery*, *werse*, and the reconstructed *ber[yinge-daye]* at line 470.

§17 The predominance of *a* before *nasals* in unlengthened (and lengthened) groups: for example, *cane*, *man*, *many*, *rane*, *woman*.

§18 OE *eo > e* in *clepe*, *flete*, *herte*, *werkes*, etc.

North Midlands forms which exclude the extreme North but indicate neither West nor East Midlands are also found.

§19 OE *ā*, ON *á > o* more often than *a*: e.g. *bones*, *clothes*, *holy*, *more*, *rode*.

---

[1] Luick §367; G. Kristensson, *A Survey of Middle English Dialects 1290–1350: The Six Northern Counties and Lincolnshire* (Lund, 1967), p. 8. M. S. Serjeantson, 'The Dialects of the West Midlands in Middle English', *RES* iii (1927), 54–67, 186–203, 319–31, lists *bonkes* as one of the few distinctive West Midlands forms but was probably relying on Gollancz's text of *Wynnere and Wastoure* where *plontes*, line 332, is emended to *bayes* (p. 331). *Bonkes* derives from ON *bakki*, and would have developed medial *-o-* through analogy.

§20 OE *ēag*, *ēah* > *egh* in *heghe*, *eghe*, etc., but we also find two examples of *hye*.

§21 OE *c̄* > *ch*: e.g. *chepe*, *childe*, *iche*, *siche*, *wirche*.

§22 OE *hw* is found only as *wh* and alliterates only with itself.

§23 The infinitive generally ends with *-e*, as *appaire*, *bere*, *drede*, *mete*, *ryde*, etc. We also find a number of forms with *-en*, as *holden*, *speken*, *swyngen*, *waxen*; or *-yn*, as *delyn*, *rewlyn*, *wepyn*; and some without ending, as *duell*, *grow*, *haf*, *tell*. However, the Midlands forms dominate.

§24 Pl. pr. indic. generally takes *-en*, as in *benden*, *clepen*, *duellen*, *liggen*, *sellen*, and so forth. We also find *delyn*, *fallyn*, *feche*, *fede*, *hafe*, *spare*, amongst others, and the *-es* forms mentioned at §9 above.

Different conclusions about the original provenance of the poem have been drawn from the linguistic evidence, although all these studies assume that the poet lived and wrote in one area. Serjeantson argues that *Wynnere and Wastoure* represents the dialect of the North Central Midlands, possibly of Nottinghamshire, 'near enough to the border of the West Midlands to account for the presence of the very rare *on*-forms for OE *a* + nasal', and Angus McIntosh has identified *Wynnere and Wastoure* as a member of a large group of texts in Thornton's two manuscripts which 'belongs somewhere not very far from where the counties of Yorkshire, Lincolnshire and Nottinghamshire meet'.[1] Offord considers *The Parlement of the Thre Ages* and, by implication, *Wynnere and Wastoure* as more northerly texts, and supports Oakden's suggestion that both poems come from an area in the extreme North-West Midlands around the Ribble boundary, possibly South Lancashire.[2] *MED*, however, includes both texts—with *William of Palerne*—as part of an East Midlands group, stressing the importance of the central counties in 'disseminating nEM features southward to the London area and in spreading EM features westward'.[3]

*Provenance*

While it may be tempting to use the variety of linguistic forms in the text to identify a precise geographical area where the poet lived and worked, this kind of research is rarely uncontroversial, as we have

---

[1] Serjeantson, p. 331; McIntosh, pp. 231–2.
[2] Offord, p. xxvi; J. P. Oakden, *Alliterative Poetry in Middle English* (2 vols., Manchester, 1930, 1935, repr. as one vol. Hamden, Connecticut, 1968), I. 52, 54–5.
[3] *MED*, 'Plan and Bibliography', p. 11.

seen, and the 'mixed dialect' of *Wynnere and Wastoure* might serve more persuasively as an indication of the author's mobility. Many forms seem to indicate the spread of the London dialect, and this evidence is notoriously difficult to interpret, but the poet's perspective is certainly national, even international, rather than provincial or regional, and his knowledge of London and court life bespeaks an involvement in contemporary urban politics. Elizabeth Salter, for example, speculates that the poem was written in honour of a member of the Wingfield family of Suffolk.[1]

More recent accounts of alliterative literature and patronage in the fourteenth century have emphasized the mobility of poets or clerks from the West Midlands attached to royal, aristocratic, or noble households, and Michael Bennett argues that the *Wynnere and Wastoure* poet was more likely one of the many 'local' men from Cheshire or Lancashire employed at the court of Westminster than a resident in these counties. If the poet were a 'careerist', to use Bennett's term, his language would very naturally reveal a mixture of dialects. Bennett's proposal also has the advantage of indicating the social context in which the poem might have been written, perhaps by a clerk in the service of one of the lords who had both estates in the North-West Midlands and connections with the court in London.[2]

*Date*

If the exact provenance of the poem is uncertain, its date is also more open to question than at any time in its critical history. In his pioneering edition of 1920, Israel Gollancz read the poem as a hastily written topical satire, directed at Edward III, the Black Prince and their management of the economic and political conditions of the winter of 1352–3.[3] In a period when medieval literature was often read as a straightforward reflection of medieval life, there was little dispute over a date which provided in *Wynnere and Wastoure* a convenient precedent in alliterative verse for *Piers Plowman*, then also regarded as a predominantly satirical work.[4] Indeed, for several decades the doubts

[1] 'The Timeliness of *Wynnere and Wastoure*', MÆ xlvii (1978), 56–9.
[2] *Community, Class and Careerism: Cheshire and Lancashire Society in the Age of Sir Gawain and the Green Knight* (Cambridge, 1983), p. 233.
[3] *A Good Short Debate Between Winner and Waster: An Alliterative Poem on Social and Economic Problems in England in the Year 1352 with Modern English Rendering*, Select Early English Poems, 3 (1920, rpt. Cambridge, 1974).
[4] T. H. Bestul surveys the debate in *Satire and Allegory in Wynnere and Wastoure* (Lincoln, Nebraska, 1974), pp. 1–3.

expressed by J. R. Hulbert were largely ignored, and discussion was confined to supplementing various details of Gollancz's dating.[1] Stillwell's identification of Wynnere with the newly powerful merchants who were in a position to finance the king's wars has been the most influential, though several unpublished works have taken up Jesse Anderson's hint that the poem is concerned with the uprising against the Black Prince in Cheshire in 1353.[2] Most agree, however, that the poem's concerns are national, not provincial. In 1978, Elizabeth Salter published an important essay which examined Gollancz's arguments from the poem's heraldic and legal references. Although she found many of his conclusions inconsistent with the evidence, she did not reject his general approach: for instance, while she refused his identification of the herald as the Black Prince, she substituted her own candidate, a member of the Wingfield family.[3]

Gollancz had read the poem as a discussion of specific events and social and economic conditions in the mid-fourteenth century, and used this internal evidence to date the poem very precisely, even though there are no unambiguous 'references' to contemporary events in the text. To give an example of his procedure, once he has interpreted the conventional picture of the king as an individualized portrait of Edward III, Gollancz then accepts the statement of Wynnere and Wastoure that they have served the king *for fyve and twenty wyntere* (l. 206) as a literal figure, and dates the poem in the twenty-fifth year of Edward's reign, 1352. He makes no allowance for the formulaic character of the number and indeed, passes over the fact that according to his own editorial policy, the line is hyper-metrical and therefore scribal. Another important aspect of Gollancz's dating is his identification of the herald who appears at line 101 as the Black Prince, Edward's son, even though there is nothing in the text to suggest any familial relationship between king and herald. Gollancz interprets the

---

[1] See J. R. Hulbert, 'The Problems of Authorship and Date of *Wynnere and Wastoure*', *MP* xviii (1920), 31–40; J. R. Steadman, 'The Date of *Wynnere and Wastoure*', *MP* xix (1921), 211–19. See also J. M. Anderson, 'A Note on the Date of *Wynnere and Wastoure*', *MLN* xliii (1928), 47–9; G. Stillwell, '*Winnere* [*sic*] *and Wastoure* and the Hundred Years' War', *ELH* viii (1941), 241–7; and D. V. Moran, '*Wynnere and Wastoure*: An Extended Footnote', *NM* lxxiii (1972), 683–5.

[2] W. B. McColly, 'The Audience of *The Parlement of the Thre Ages* and *Wynnere and Wastoure*' (Ph.D., UCLA, 1957); and L. M. Rosenfield, '*Wynnere and Wastoure*: A Critical Edition' (Ph.D., Columbia, 1975).

[3] E. Salter (1978). In the same year, David A. Lawton also raised doubts about the date of *Wynnere and Wastoure*, and suggested that it was influenced by *Piers Plowman*: 'Literary History and Scholarly Fancy: The Date of Two Middle English Alliterative Poems', *Parergon*, xviii (1977), 17–25.

herald's coat of arms as those of the Black Prince, and although this argument is quite attenuated, as Salter demonstrates, he emends the herald's speech at line 108, rejecting the manuscript reading *Ʒis lorde* for the hypothetical *Y serue, lorde*. Gollancz thus introduces into the poem an English version of the Black Prince's motto, *Ich dene*, a conjecture which has seemed to confirm the herald's identity for many readers.[1]

Even if one accepts Gollancz's interpretative premise that the poem is a topical and timely work, the inaccuracy and inconsistency of many of his arguments for the poem's date should discount them from serious consideration.[2] For example, if the situation in the poem is supposed to mirror the events of the winter of 1352–3, Gollancz needs to explain why the poet presents the king as *planning* to march on Paris, whereas in fact, the king had been in France from September 1352 and would remain there until hostilities recommenced in March of the following year.[3] Again, while other less specific references in the poem to political or economic conditions can be made to fit this year, such as general 'questions of labour, wages, prices, dress, food' which recall the Statute of Labourers of 1351, and 'allusions to questions resulting from the Black Death of 1349', Gollancz explains that the Black Death and its tragic after-effects are not specifically mentioned because 'they belonged to the immediate past, and their effects were obvious'. The circularity of Gollancz's argument is soon apparent, and it is similarly hard to account for the high praise of the king and prince in a poem which is read, in part, as being critical of their government.

There is no doubt of course that the poem does allude to contemporary conditions, and subsequent scholarship has deepened our understanding of the mid-century context of the poem. Gollancz is right, for example, to draw our attention to the labour shortages after the Black Death and the consequent problems of vagrancy, the prevalence of criminal gangs of different classes, and the various Statutes introduced to inhibit their activity—the Statute of Labourers (1351)

---

[1] Salter, pp. 49–50. See also Commentary.

[2] Salter analyses each of Gollancz's arguments in detail, and the reader is referred to this thorough study for a fuller discussion than is possible here.

[3] Indeed, this factor made Gollancz reluctant to date the poem in 1352–53 until 1920. See his earlier discussions in his edition of *The Parlement of the Thre Ages* (Roxburghe Club, cxxxii, London, 1897) in which *Wynnere and Wastoure* is printed as an Appendix, and in two notes on *Wynnere and Wastoure*, in *The Athenaeum*, 24 Aug., cxviii (1901), 254–5 and 14 Sept., cxviii (1901), 351. He had also wanted to date the poem earlier than 1350 to account for its failure to refer to the Black Death.

and the Treasons Statute (1352)—and the role of Sir William Shareshull (mentioned at line 317) in drafting some of this legislation. Stillwell's discussion of Edward III's dependence on the merchants in Parliament to finance his overseas wars sheds considerable light on the characterization of Wynnere, but none of these 'allusions' fixes a date at 1352–3. The appearance of the Garter motto on the king's pavilion similarly dates the poem after 1348 when the Order of the Garter was instituted, but we are reminded that the poet of *Sir Gawain and the Green Knight* also quotes the motto in the last years of the century. 1352 can be only a *terminus a quo* for *Wynnere and Wastoure.* Gollancz had insisted in his Preface, though, that the poet was writing 'concerning events which are just happening, or are fresh in his memory. His poem is in fact a topical pamphlet in alliterative verse on the social and economic problems of the hour, as vivid as present-day discussions on like problems.'[1]

I have argued elsewhere that Gollancz is especially concerned to trace these parallels between England in 1352 and 1920, and that part of his enthusiasm for the poem is motivated by his own post-war patriotism.[2] It also seems clear that his argument for the poem's date and internal references is now inseparable from his heavily emended edition, and a new text of the poem is the first step in a reassessment of these questions.

My contention is that Gollancz's dating seeks precision where it cannot be found, and that the limits should be set at 1352–c. 1370.[3] I agree with Gollancz *contra* Salter that the herald's words at lines 126–9 refer to the Treasons Statute of 1352, but it is only because Shareshull's name appears later in the poem that the phrase *his pese to distourbe* seems significant. When the herald addresses the two armies, he charges them on penalty of death and forfeiture of their land that they do not move a step closer

> To lede rowte in his rewme so ryall to thynke,
> Pertly with ȝoure powers his pese to disturbe.
>
> (lines 128–9)

---

[1] Gollancz, p. xii. (The page numbers in the reprinted edition are missing: I count from the first printed page.)

[2] 'Israel Gollancz's *Wynnere and Wastoure*: Political Satire or Editorial Politics?', in *Medieval English Religious and Ethical Literature: Essays in Honour of George H. Russell*, ed. Gregory Kratzmann and James Simpson (Cambridge, 1986), pp. 115–27.

[3] So also Lawton, 'Middle English Alliterative Poetry: An Introduction', in *Middle English Alliterative Poetry and its Literary Background*, ed. Lawton (Cambridge, 1982), p. 3 n. 8.

Much later in the debate, Wastoure complains against Shareshull (lines 317–18) who had accused him of precisely the same offence, *That saide I prikkede with powere his pese to distourbe.* Clearly this phrase, 'disturbing the peace' is linked quite precisely for the poet with the practice of leading armed bands, and the legislative attempts to curb this activity. As Salter points out, though, if the herald's speech is intended to echo the terms of the Statute, it is a rather confused echo which conflates the distinctions between high treason, petty treason, and felony that the Statute was designed to enforce. The herald threatens them with the punishment for high treason, which would have been appropriate under the Statute only if Wynnere and Wastoure had been marching against the king, not each other: this was an activity specifically defined by the act as felony or trespass, not treason.[1]

Even so, the issues raised by the Statute were topical for several decades—as the many complaints about bastard feudalism under Richard II testify—and if the poet were writing at a later date or did not intend an accurate legal reference, he may not have been so concerned to replicate its terms exactly. The poet later has Wastoure employ Shareshull's name as a term of abuse, and this would surely have currency as long as the unpopular Chief Justice was still alive, and an approximate *terminus ad quem* is thus provided by Shareshull's death by 1370 or perhaps even a few years later.[2]

Further alleged references in the poem to contemporary figures and conditions are vague in comparison, and while they can help us read the poem in its general context, they cannot help us date it more precisely.

The date of *Wynnere and Wastoure* has been a significant issue for our understanding not only of the poem itself but also its place in the development of alliterative poetry in the fourteenth century. The poet seems to draw on a well-established and highly polished style of unrhymed alliterative composition; and in many accounts of alliterative poetry *Wynnere and Wastoure* is used to exemplify the tradition against which Langland is said to have defined his own poetic style, that is by adopting its moral concerns, its topography and some of its characters, but modifying the 'excesses' of the alliterative high style, especially its vocabulary. Conversely, in the uncertainty about the date

---

[1] Salter, pp. 41–3.
[2] Hulbert had taken 1366 as a *terminus ad quem*, the year in which Shareshull's commission of oyer and terminer was revoked (Hulbert, 1920), pp. 35–7.

of our poem, David Lawton suggests that this line of influence be reversed.[1] The comparative poetic and metrical informality of *Piers Plowman* would thus take on a new light, once Langland is credited with forming a distinctive poetic style out of the various kinds of alliterative writing current in the fourteenth century (the 'continuum' of which Pearsall writes),[2] while the *Wynnere and Wastoure* poet develops a more elaborate style. However, we should resist substituting one simple line of influence for another: even if we could be sure of the dates of both works, neither poem alone can account for all the stylistic features of the other. In any case, our ignorance of this early stage of unrhymed alliterative poetry is still great, and although it is tempting to shift the emphasis onto *Piers Plowman* because we know so much more about its literary sources (its dependence on the homiletic tradition, for example), a full study of Langland's poem in its metrical context has yet to be made.

## METRE

### Alliterative Metre

Modern studies in alliterative poetry have taken two main directions, each with implications for editorial practice, and we are reminded that the metre of any alliterative poem must always be considered in conjunction with a study of editorial policy. Against a background of conflicting theories about the origin and development of alliterative metre in the fourteenth century, recent editors have tended to favour conservative editorial policies, especially in earlier poems where, it is argued, the metre may still be developing.[3] On the other hand, it has been contended that most variations on the normative pattern of three alliterating stresses per line (aa/ax) are scribally introduced. Hoyt Duggan

---

[1] Lawton (1977); and 'The Unity of Middle English Alliterative Poetry', *Speculum*, lviii (1983), 80–1.

[2] D. A. Pearsall, *Old English and Middle English Poetry* (London, 1977), p. 150; and 'The Origins of the Alliterative Revival', in *The Alliterative Tradition in the Fourteenth Century*, ed. B. S. Levy and P. E. Szarmach (Kent, Ohio, 1981), 1–24.

[3] Some of the most important modern contributions to this debate are N. F. Blake, 'Rhythmical Alliteration', *MP* lxvii (1969), 118–24; T. Turville-Petre, *The Alliterative Revival* (Cambridge, 1977), and Blake's review, 'Middle English Alliterative Revivals', *Review*, i (1979), 205–14; E. Salter, 'Alliterative Modes and Affiliations in the Fourteenth Century', *NM* lxxix (1978), 25–35; D. Pearsall (1981); and articles by Lawton, McIntosh, and Pearsall in Lawton (ed.) (1982). See in particular Lawton's edition of *Joseph of Arimathie*, in which it is argued that the surviving text represents an early draft (New York and London, 1983).

and Thorlac Turville-Petre have examined those poems which survive in more than one manuscript, while Duggan suggests that all the
alliterative poets wrote within 'a single, remarkably stable poetic'.
Both would encourage the restoration of this metrical pattern in the
majority of alliterative texts, whether they survive in one or several
manuscripts.[1]

A detailed account of this scholarship would be beyond the scope of
the present volume; nor is it possible to consider the different des-
criptive accounts or theories of the alliterative line. Many studies of
this kind nevertheless share a methodological flaw which to a large
extent vitiates their conclusions. Following Oakden and perhaps
ultimately Sievers, prosodists have worked by classifying types of
alliterative lines, and comparing statistics of their comparative use and
frequency in different poems. At best, this method can sometimes
reveal anomalies and stylistic differences between poets, but at worst,
can lead the prosodist to consider the poetry only in terms of abstract
patterns, regardless of the manner in which a poet must use metrical
variation to establish and resolve tension between stress, syntax,
sense, rhythm, and, in this case, alliteration. R. W. Sapora, for
example, attempts a generative analysis of Middle English alliterative
metre as a way of predicting stylistic variation within a poem and
between different poems. He rarely examines a given line in its own
metrical context, though, and does not consider the role of unstressed
syllables in the line.[2]

Such paradigmatic studies—to borrow Saussure's term—should be
taken in conjunction with a syntagmatic reading of the poetry.[3] It is
essential to recognize that alliterative variation can produce different
and complex rhythmical sequences in a series of lines, and perhaps
more importantly, that a heteromorphic verse form must always work
by establishing a rhythmical pattern, varying it and then resolving it.[4]
For example, the *Wynnere and Wastoure* poet, like the poet of the *Morte*

---

[1] T. Turville-Petre, 'Emendation on Grounds of Alliteration in *The Wars of Alexander*', *ES* lxi (1980), 302–17; H. N. Duggan, 'The Shape of the B-Verse in Middle English
Alliterative Poetry', *Speculum*, lxi (1986), 564–92; and 'Alliterative Patterning as a Basis
for Emendation in Middle English Alliterative Poetry', *SAC* viii (1986), 73–104.

[2] *A Theory of Middle English Alliterative Metre with Critical Applications. Speculum Anniversary Monographs*, vii (Cambridge, Mass., 1977). Sapora's policy of relying on texts edited
according to different metrical principles also produces inconsistent results.

[3] F. de Saussure, *Course in General Linguistics*, ed. C. Bally and A. Sechehaye in col-
laboration with A. Riedlinger, trans., introd. W. Baskin (New York, 1959), pp. 122–7.

[4] The term is recommended by McIntosh, 'Early Middle English Alliterative Verse',
in Lawton (ed.) (1982), pp. 21–2.

*Arthure*, uses alliterative linking or couplet alliteration to allow greater variety or lighter alliteration within a single line, and it is variation of just this kind which is obscured when alliterative and metrical patterns are studied in isolation from their rhythmical contexts.[1]

Similarly, Duggan argues from manuscript evidence that the b-verse pattern xx/xx/(x) was avoided by the poets. His comparisons of the manuscripts are suggestive, but they do not prove conclusively that all poets rejected this pattern: there is no intrinsic reason why this should be unacceptable, nor indeed any evidence that the poets were accustomed to counting syllables.[2]

It is also worth reminding ourselves that most poems of the alliterative corpus have editorial histories of considerable re-writing and regularizing, and it is often difficult to read the metrical forms preserved in a manuscript without finding them deficient in comparison with early editions of the poems. Thus the other pitall to avoid is that of using a preconceived notion of metrical regularity in assessing alliterative lines.

In this study I have assumed two things: first, that the alliterative metre of the fourteenth century represents a new development, one which draws on an older 'continuum' of alliterative writing in prose and poetry; and second, that we are not justified in assuming an unbroken oral or 'popular' tradition from Old English metre. Many scholars further assume that all the fourteenth-century poets wrote according to the same rules; but it seems far more likely, given the geographical and chronological distances involved and the presumed isolation of many poets, that each wrote with his own understanding of the metre, and evolved his own rules and licences. The poets whose works survive do seem to have worked within a basic grammar of alliterative composition which employed various syntactic frames and expressions.[3] None the less, it is reasonable to assume degrees of competency within that grammar, which may itself have varied from place to place, and time to time. Therefore, while comparisons with other poets' use of alliteration and metrical patterns can be instructive when reading a given poem, the most important data must be the evidence of the manuscripts.

[1] See J. L. N. O'Loughlin, 'The Middle English Alliterative *Morte Arthure*', MÆ iv (1935), 153–68.

[2] Duggan, *Speculum* (1986).

[3] See, for example, Joan Turville-Petre, 'The Metre of *Sir Gawain and the Green Knight*', ES lvii (1976), 310–28; R. A. Waldron, 'Oral-formulaic Technique and Middle English Alliterative Poetry', *Speculum*, xxxii (1957), 792–804.

## Thornton as Copyist

In editing a single manuscript copy, we are necessarily quite depend-
ent on the scribe. Fortunately, Thornton seems to have had a strong
sense of responsibility to his exemplars. He was presumably not working under supervision, but on a number of occasions he can be
observed checking his text against his exemplar and correcting his
own work. There remain a considerable number of copying errors,
ranging from the confusion of one or more letter forms to the large-
scale repetition of up to twenty lines in texts of other poems. Even so,
the frequency with which Thornton becomes aware of his error gives
us some grounds for confidence, especially since he corrects larger
errors by drawing a single line through the offending reading, so that
most remain legible. In the text of *Wynnere and Wastoure*, for instance, a
word or phrase in the second half of the line is sometimes cancelled
with a single stroke and then corrected (16, 50, 184, 195, 224, 274, 348).[1]
Three of these examples seem to indicate his unconscious substitution of a synonymous phrase to produce the final, non-alliterating
stress in the line. These readings (*one hande* for *neghe aftir* at line 16,
*attyred* for *full brighte* at line 50, *blyn* for *thynken* at line 195 and possibly
the uncorrected anticipation of 95b at 94b) would make minimal difference to the sense of the lines, yet Thornton reveals a scrupulous
attention to detail in correcting them. By the same token, however, his
ready assimilation of the alliterative cadence alerts us to the likelihood
that his text may also feature uncorrected scribal forms in this position, either accidental or deliberate. Be that as it may, the cancelled
readings make little difference either to style or sense, and it seems
that Thornton was motivated by a strong sense of faithfulness to his
exemplar. Mary Hamel, who has examined Thornton's corrections to
his text of the *Morte Arthure* in the Lincoln manuscript, finds similar
tendencies there, and adds that 'a stressed word is over three times as
likely to show an error of some kind as an unstressed word'.[2]

At other times, a word is omitted from the text but later supplied in
the margin, with the correct position indicated (143, 321, 390). More
often, though, one or more letters are written over others (38, 91, 94,
179, 181, 419). All but two of these examples of self-correction are

---

[1] All these examples of self-correction are noted in the apparatus to the text.
[2] 'Scribal Self-Corrections in the Thornton *Morte Arthure*', *SB* xxxvi (1983), 130.
Hamel also suggests that Thornton is more likely to respell a word in the first than in
the second half-line, and in staves than in unstressed words (p. 136). The vast majority
of examples in *Wynnere and Wastoure* occurs in the b-verse, however.

found in the first 352 lines, written at apparently greater leisure in single columns, and we can assume that Thornton checked his work more thoroughly on these leaves. His corrections are invaluable as a guide to the detection of other errors in his text: as we have seen, his characteristic errors are confusion of letter forms, omission of a word, anticipation of a reading that appears later in the line and unconscious substitution of a word or phrase.

## The Metre of Wynnere and Wastoure

Before any attempt is made to correct the text, or conjecture about the lines damaged by the tear on the last leaf of the manuscript, it is necessary to identify the poetic licences and variations the poet seems to allow to the basic shape of his line, and to determine under what stylistic or rhythmical conditions he would permit these licences. Of course it is not always possible to distinguish the poet's original work from scribal re-writing; nevertheless the vast majority of lines in *Wynnere and Wastoure* that seem free from obvious mechanical copying errors or deliberate scribal re-writing conform to the same alliterative pattern. These lines can be used to isolate a metrical 'grammar', or a set of minimum requirements for alliteration; and the lines that fail to fulfil these requirements will be either deliberate stylistic exceptions or examples of scribal corruption.

The most common line type has four or five major stresses, three of which alliterate together. Two of these stresses fall in a shorter half-line after a mid-line break of varying syntactic and rhythmic weight. This second half-line tends to be the more formulaic and rhythmically regular, and the whole line thus partakes of a falling cadence, as the rhythmical and syntactical complexities of the first half of the line are usually resolved in the second half. For example, while the b-verse commonly takes the form /ax, the a-verse can range from aa/, aaa/, xaa/, axa/, to aax/, and the poet can also vary the degree of stress. There is further scope for different patterns in the number and disposition of unstressed syllables in the a-verse.

In the list of minimum requirements for an alliterative line that follows, I have not assumed that alliteration must fall on the initial syllable of a word or must always be supported by a major rhythmical stress, as Gollancz, and many other editors of alliterative poetry have done. Line 198, *That ʒe wend with me are any wrake falle*, for example, is considered here as a regular line, although Gollancz corrects it to reconcile alliteration with stress, *That ʒe wend [me with]*. . . . It is admittedly difficult to be certain of the stress certain syllables would have received in Middle English, and it is important to read these lines in their metrical contexts. Yet in comparison with other poets who allow prepositions or verbs of light syntactic weight as vehicles of alliteration, the author of *Wynnere and Wastoure* appears to be quite strict: he usually allows only one lightly stressed (or occasionally, unstressed) word in each line to bear alliteration and in contrast to Langland, only in the first and heavier half of the line, which can more easily accommodate and compensate for this weakness.[1]

The following rules, then, seem to govern the alliteration in each line:

(1) Alliteration may fall on the letters *b*, *c*, *ch*, *d*, *g*, *ʒ*, *h*, *j*, *k*, *l*, *m*, *n*, *p*, *r*, *s*, *t*, *th*, *w* and *wh*. Vowels may alliterate with other vowels but not with *h*. *Qu* < OE *cw*, OF *qu* does not alliterate with *wh* < OE *hw*.

(2) Each line must have a minimum of three alliterating syllables, two of which must coincide with stressed syllables. One of these must be the stress after the midline break.

These rules could be formulated in different ways, but they can be used to group together 477 of the poem's 503 lines which can thus be described as *alliterating* to the pattern aa/ax, with the important proviso that this represents a minimum requirement, not an exclusive group of lines which produce an identical rhythmical effect. Oakden, for example, uses aa/ax to designate the *total* rhythmic and alliterative structure of a line, often with very reductive results.

Many lines of our poem thus fulfil these minimum requirements, which might otherwise be represented as aax/ax, e.g. *ʒarked alle of ʒalowe golde in full ʒape wyse* (75), axa/ax, e.g. *A brod chechun at þe bakke þe breste had anoþer* (116) or, where (a) denotes alliteration falling on a lighter stress: (a)xa/ax e.g. *ʒe hafe no myster of the helpe of þe heuen kyng* (361); a(a)x/ax e.g. *For dyn of the depe watir and dadillyng of fewllys* (44); or lines with double alliteration: aab/ab e.g. *Roste with the riche sewes and the ryalle spyces* (339), since the alliteration on *r* obeys all the rules above. Also included are many lines which exceed the minimum

---

[1] The lines affected are 3, 47, 67, 79, 85, 198, 277, 310, 316, 335. Line 101, *The kyng biddith a beryn by hym þat stondeth*, alliterates on a preposition after a mid-line break, but in this case *by* might receive greater emphasis than the pronoun *hym*. Line 125, which alliterates only once in the first half line on an unstressed syllable, is excluded from this larger category, and is discussed below.

alliterative requirements: e.g. aaa/ax *When wawes waxen schall wilde and walles bene doun* (12); and the single example of aa/aa alliteration at line 167, *That was Domynyke this daye with dynttis to dele.*

Great variety is possible within these minimum constraints, of course, and many features such as the counterpointing of rhythm, alliteration and stress (especially in the longer a-verses), or the use of different patterns of unstressed or lightly stressed syllables become apparent only in the context of a given line. The poet varies his rhythm considerably, always balancing a longer b-verse, for example, with a regular form in the following line. It is certainly rare to find long sequences of consecutive lines or half-lines sharing the same rhythmic pattern or number of unstressed syllables between stresses. The poet either varies the relationship between stress and alliteration or, less noticeably, the number of unstressed syllables in the line.

Such repetition is occasionally exploited for rhetorical emphasis, however. Compare lines 231–2 and the poet's use of *definitio*:

> I gedir, I glene and he lattys goo sone
> I pryke and I pryne and he the purse opynes.

Compare also lines 349–54, part of Wynnere's mouth-watering description of Wastoure's feast, where the lavishness of the menu is emphasized by the similar shape of the a-verses. The poet employs a number of stylistic variations such as alliterative couplets; ornamental linking between lines, which might be represented as aa/ab: bb/bx (e.g. lines 8–9, 20–1); and sequences of several lines alliterating on a few letters, in rapid alternation. Lines 280–7, for example, alliterate on *w, f, w, w, l, k, l, f,* with linking between lines 285–6 and constant alliterative echoes throughout. More of these structural and ornamental subtleties—if such a distinction can be maintained—reveal themselves on successive readings of the poem, and would certainly reward a more detailed study than is possible here.

As we have seen, 477 lines conform to this basic pattern. The alliterative patterns of five of the remaining lines (353, 354, 355, 358, 471) have been disturbed by the damage to the last leaf on the manuscript. That leaves twenty-one lines which do not conform to the rules outlined above. Our task is now to assess whether these lines represent authorial variation or scribal corruption, to enable editorial reconstruction, particularly of the damaged lines.

Mechanical error accounts for two lines: it is safe to assume the accidental omission of a word, almost certainly *hert*, in line 454, while confusion between letter forms has given *layren* for *kayre*[*n*] in line 502 (see Commentary).

Two lines seem to feature alliteration between voiced and unvoiced consonants, and might thus be reclassified as aa/ax lines:

334 Venyson with the frumentee and fesanttes full riche
362 þus are 3e scorned by skyll and schathed þeraftir

Neither line seems defective in sense, and since neither *sch* nor *sc*, *sk* forms an exclusive alliterating consonantal group, line 362 could also be described as alliterating aa/ax on *s*.

Voiced and unvoiced consonants alliterate in two further lines which would otherwise be aa/xx lines:

275 For þe colde wyntter and þe kene with gleterand frostes
332 The bores hede schall be broghte with plontes appon lofte.

In fact Gollancz emends both these lines while preserving the manuscript reading at 334 and 362. Yet lines 275 and 332 form alliterating couplets with the preceding or following line, and I have assumed that this represents a deliberate device of stylistic variation.

Line 423, *Than þe Wastour wrothly castes vp his eghne*, has also been rejected as scribal by some editors, but it offers a similarly strong reading and forms a couplet alliterating on *w* with the following line.

There are four other lines alliterating aa/xx which are rejected as scribal, since they violate the basic rules of alliterative composition, without forming couplets:

79 And two out of Ynglonde with sex grym bestes
121 He brake a braunche in his hande and caughten it swythe
314 And thies beryns one the bynches with howes one lofte
369 What sall lympe of þe, lede, within fewe 3eris.

Other lines (132, 429) offer only two alliterating stresses on the pattern ax/ax, but it is difficult to detect mechanical error, and they are surrounded on both sides by regular rhythms and alliterative echoes. Compare,

If any **b**eryn **b**e so **b**olde with **b**anere for to **r**yde
Withinn þe **k**yngdome **r**iche bot the **k**ynge one
That he schall **l**osse the **l**onde and his **l**yfe aftir.

(131–3)

It lyes wele for a lede his lemman to fynde
Aftir hir faire chere to forthir hir herte.
Then will scho loue hym lelely as hir lyfe one. . . .
(428–30)

There are three examples of xa/ax alliteration at lines 125, 177, and 266. Even though the single alliterating syllable in the a-verse of line 125, *Send his erande by me als hym beste lyketh*, falls on the preposition *by*, the line forms part of a couplet on *b* with the following line, and the alliterative pattern is retained in the text (see Commentary). Lines 177, *For þay are the ordire þat louen oure lady to serue* and 266, *In playinge and in wakynge in wynttres nyghttis*, do not share alliterating syllables with surrounding lines, and are suspected of scribal corruption on other grounds: both are emended in the text.

The pattern aa/xa appears twice in the manuscript where the sense in the second half line seems to have been inverted for extra emphasis or variety: line 197, *Forthi I bid ȝow bothe that thaym hedir broghte*, and 356, ⟨. . .⟩*e a mese at a merke bytwen twa men*. In fact, the incomplete line 471 is emended to this pattern (see Commentary).

There is one instance of ax/aa alliteration at line 103, *Thynke I dubbede the knyghte with dynttis to dele*. Again, it seems reasonable to assume this is introduced for variety: perhaps the poet wanted to add interest to a line which featured a very familiar phrase.[1]

Several other anomalous patterns appear which involve double alliteration: aaa/bb at 386, *And fisches flete in þe flode and ichone ete oþer*, and ba/ab at 476, *Where any potet beryn þurgh þe burgh passe*. The first pattern, where three alliterating stresses occur before the midline break, is a licence allowed by Langland, who often makes no attempt to add the compensating factor of double alliteration in the second half. And we note that line 476 also features the alliteration of voiced and unvoiced consonants.[2]

To sum up, then, the metrical evidence suggests that the *Wynnere and Wastoure* poet will allow lines to alliterate on the pattern aa/xx only when part of a couplet or when voiced and unvoiced alliteration is involved (lines 423, 275, 362). Lines 79, 121, 314, and 369 which alliterate aa/xx without fulfilling these conditions are emended in the text as they seem to have suffered mechanical scribal error or deliberate substitution. The pattern ax/ax, where the alliterating syllables are

---

[1] Duggan, however, would usually only allow this pattern when the alliteration falls on vowels. See 'The Shape of the B-Verse', p. 569.

[2] *Potet* is problematic in sense, however, and is emended to *petit* in the text.

evenly distributed across the line, is allowed as a variant (lines 132, 429) but xa/ax, where they are clustered in the middle, must form part of a couplet (line 125). Other examples at lines 177 and 266 are almost certainly scribal and are corrected. The pattern aa/xa is allowed at lines 197 and 356, and ax/aa at line 103. Unusual patterns of double alliteration on aaa/bb and ab/ba are preserved at lines 386 and 476. It is doubtful whether the poet ever formulated these variations as rules or principles: nevertheless, they indicate the degree of variation from his standard line which he was prepared to consider as metrical in particular contexts.

As far as the number of unstressed syllables in the line is concerned, the poets presumably did not count these consciously. Gollancz emended many lines of *Wynnere and Wastoure* on the assumption that each b-verse should feature a two-syllable dip, though more recent editors have been reluctant to tamper with numbers of unstressed syllables, since this is not, after all, a syllabic metre. Duggan, however, suggests that the pattern xx/xx/(x) was regarded as unacceptable in the b-verse of *The Siege of Jerusalem*, *The Wars of Alexander*, and *The Parlement of the Thre Ages* and that therefore editors of alliterative poetry can feel confident in correcting all instances of such lines. But regardless of Duggan's assumptions about the uniformity of poetical practice, there are no intrinsic reasons why this pattern should be unacceptable. Certainly no one had noticed it as aberrant, until it was revealed as a statistically light phenomenon. This pattern appears twelve times in the manuscript of *Wynnere and Wastoure*, and indeed, line 372 *Ay to appaire þe pris and* [*it*] *passe nott to hye*, has been emended to fit this pattern. Nine of these lines feature a rising rhythm in the a-verse, so that the last stress of the a-verse and the first of the b-verse are separated by only two unstressed syllables, and the rhythm is by no means intrusive or irregular (cf. lines 47, 57, 148, etc.). Once more, though Duggan's comparisons of the manuscripts are suggestive, they are not conclusive proof that all poets rejected this line pattern.

## SUMMARY

*Lines 1 – 30: Prologue*

The prologue introduces the authoritative, anonymous voice of the narrator, a Western man who is apprehensive of London and the court, and jealous of their influence on younger generations. His age and experience lend authority to his prophetic utterances and qualify him to offer advice to lords through his poetry, though he laments that good poetry and wise counsel are too often ignored.

### Lines 31–69: The Meadow and the Dream-Landscape

The debate is framed by two settings, a mysterious meadow in which the narrator falls asleep and a dream-landscape which combines formal and structural elements from the medieval theatre and tournament. The meadow is recognizable as an example of the lush and fertile *locus amœnus* which often figures as the dream-landscape in medieval poetry. In describing the landscape of his vision the poet draws on the conventions of the medieval theatre and those of the joust or tournament, for the king will be cast as the judge. Two armies march towards each other, ready to fight.

### Lines 70–120: The Wodwyse, King and Herald

Three figures are introduced, a man dressed as a *wodwyse*, or wild man, who stands on the cliff, wearing a helmet and mantling which bears the royal arms of England. A knight stands by the king's pavilion, but the king himself is described first, dressed in elaborate robes, and seated wearing his crown and carrying a sceptre. He speaks to the knight who attends him, and commands him to prevent the armies from joining battle. The herald arms himself as if for battle, and the narrator praises him as a worthy and promising young man.

### Lines 121–201: The Herald's Speech

The herald takes a branch as a symbol of peace, and makes his way towards the armies. He delivers the king's message, forbidding them to engage in any further hostilities and threatening them with death and forfeiture of their property. Because they are ignorant of the king and his customs, however, he assures them of forgiveness. He then describes both armies, but does not identify their leaders. The armies are drawn from France, Lorraine, Lombardy, Spain, Westphalia, England, and Ireland, while many *Estirlynges*, or merchants from East Germany, are also present. The herald blazons some of the banners of one army: here are ranged the pope, a group of lawyers, and the four orders of friars, supported by groups of merchants. On the opposite side is a strong army of archers, though we learn little more about them other than that they are ready and willing to fight.

### Lines 202–20: The King's Household

The two leaders emerge from their armies and inform the herald that they are in the king's service. They accompany him on horseback, ascend the *clyffe* on foot and kneel before the king who welcomes them courteously, acknowledging them as servants of his household. Wynnere and Wastoure are not distinguished by their physical appearance or demeanour but are described as *knyghtis full comly*. The king calls for wine and the narrator steps in to tell us that it seemed to him that he drank deeply of the wine, as the first fitt ends.

### Lines 221–45: Wynnere's First Speech

Wynnere opens with an attack on his opponent. Firstly, however, he introduces himself as a man who works towards the common good, *a wy that alle this werlde helpis*, staking his claim for total responsibility for economic management. Wynnere claims to teach lords how to manage their wealth by living parsimoniously, attempting to preclude the charge of avarice by naming Witt as a mentor. Wynnere presents himself as a moderate and Wastoure as an extremist, his own economic programme as sufficient for the kingdom, and Wastoure's as personally sinful and detrimental to social stability—a strategy adopted by both disputants. Wynnere accuses Wastoure of pride, and vents his frustration at the latter's neglect of his property, which has fallen into unprofitable ruin. Perhaps worst of all, Wastoure is guilty of abusing his aristocratic station, of riding about on his own pleasure and failing to fulfil his duty. Wynnere concludes by predicting economic ruin for the country unless Wastoure is destroyed, and asks that they be permitted to settle their differences in battle.

### Lines 246–62: Wastoure's First Speech

Wastoure opens by mocking Wynnere's anger, one of the few debating techniques that distinguish him from his opponent. Both are consistently angry and vehement, yet where Wynnere is sober and gloomy, Wastoure is buoyant and defiant. He abuses Wynnere for stockpiling wool, bacon, and money which will never be used, invoking a tradi-

tional figure of ethical satire, the avaricious merchant who canno
sleep for anxiety about his goods. In asking his rhetorical question at
line 253, *'What scholde worthe of that wele if no waste come?'*, Wastoure
presents his policy as the healthy and grateful consumption of God's
bounty, the proper use of Wastoure's hoarded wealth. In effect,
Wastoure claims that Wynnere relies on his services, and their mutual
interdependence will become an important theme in the debate.
Wastoure then appeals to the plight of the poor, telling Wynnere he
has condemned himself to be hanged in hell for neglecting them.

### *Lines 263–93: Wynnere's Second Speech*

Wynnere disdains defence, but keeps up the attack on wasting, which
he now associates with pride, gluttony, and lechery. Wynnere also
claims that any food shortages among the poor are Wastoure's responsibility, since he has consumed all the wealth of the kingdom through
his feasting and irresponsible behaviour, while his followers have sold
their inheritances to buy luxurious clothing. Wastoure is also guilty of
neglecting the natural agricultural cycles and the traditional farming
methods of his ancestors; he courts his own damnation by spending
his time in the tavern, and indulging in indiscriminate sexual promiscuity. Wynnere exhorts him to set his estates in order and threatens
him with hellfire.

### *Lines 294–323: Wastoure's Second Speech*

Wastoure precedes his first full-scale attack by defending lavish
spending as pleasing to God and the most appropriate use of wealth in
the public interest. By contrast, Wynnere hoards private, individual
wealth which no one will ever use, for his fortune will be dissipated
after his death in lawsuits his son and executors will bring against each
other, or carried off by friars in last minute bequests. Wastoure warns
Wynnere that leaving money to the poor in his will is no guarantee
against eternal damnation: almsgiving should be a constant part of the
rich man's life.

   Wastoure then rails against restrictive authority of every kind and
against any limitation to excess. He condemns Wynnere and Wanhope, his associate, and wishes them drowned, along with all fast days
and saints' eves, revealing his own extremism by condemning fast days
as parsimonious. Wastoure would then put *dedly synn* to trial for their

death and introduces the main object of his attack, the legal profession and in particular, Judge Shareshull. He then appeals to proverbial wisdom to prove Wynnere's cowardice, and agrees that they should resolve the debate through battle.

### Lines 324–67: Wynnere's Third Speech

Wynnere angrily tries to capitalize on Wastoure's outburst, attempting to discredit him with an account of the company he keeps and the extravagance with which he entertains them. No members of the nobility eat with him, but only a few henchmen who owe him a favour. Wynnere's description of Wastoure's highly extravagant menu becomes ever more tantalizing and attractive as, inspired by envy, his eloquence increases. He describes his own meagre fare of salt beef and vegetables, with the exception of *ane hene to hym that the howse owethe*, a reference, perhaps, to the modest food he will serve his lord, and we recall that we witness a debate between two servants of the king's household.

Again, the narrator calls for drinks at the end of the second fitt.

### Lines 368–91: Wastoure's Third Speech

Wastoure moves into a serious and impassioned attack, presenting himself as the stabilizing element in society, responsible for maintaining the appropriate and natural social and economic hierarchies, while Wynnere perversely attempts to make personal profit out of scarcity. He is accused of hoping for a bad harvest so that as prices rise, he may profit from grain he has stored in a previous year, but if the harvest is good after all, Wynnere will wish to take his own life in despair.

Wastoure claims it is both appropriate and desirable for lords to spend money and consume the produce of their estates: if not, food will become more plentiful, they will not be able to attract any servants, and the social hierarchy will be disturbed. Wastoure promises improved conditions for the poor, although it is not immediately obvious how this will come about. His tone becomes almost conspiratorial, *þis wate þou full wele witterly þiseluen*, as he appeals to Wynnere's own conservatism. Wastoure ends by affirming Wynnere's dependence on him.

*Lines 392–422: Wynnere's Fourth Speech*

In his final attack, Wynnere criticizes the practicality of Wastoure's scheme, saying that the very poor will never be able to buy furs or silk-covered saddles: their share of Wastoure's wealth will be pathetically small. In any case, to please their wives, the nobility have squandered their wealth with no thought of investing for the future, selling their land and despoiling their forests. Wynnere reminisces nostalgically about the gracious lifestyle enjoyed by Wastoure's ancestors, while Wastoure and his followers have abandoned the dignity proper to their station, and spend their money on pleasure and luxury, flirting with expensive fashions. Wynnere draws the powerful contrast of the Virgin in her flight into Egypt, an exemplum of humility and poverty. Whatever the force of Wynnere's previous arguments, this strategy is just about unanswerable, and Wastoure's sole recourse is to attack his hypocrisy.

*Lines 423–53: Wastoure's Fourth Speech*

Wastoure argues vehemently but inconsistently in his final speech. At first he presents himself as financially independent of Wynnere (*What hafe our clothes coste þe, caytef, to by?*), and answers his criticism that he has neglected traditional values with a sentimental evocation of the courtly love ethic and the ennobling effects of courtship on the lover. He defends the fine clothes of his supporters as expenditure that brings him honour, following this with a startling contrast between the virtuous activity of his supporters in winning the love of their ladies and the sloth and complacency of Wynnere's caution and circumspection, boldly condemned as a waste of time. Once more Wastoure predicts the fate of the miser's fortune, which will never reach the hands of those to whom it has been bequeathed. He closes his speech on a characteristically confused, quick-tempered note, in dramatic contrast with Wynnere's sober conclusion. Contradicting his earlier praise of the labours of love, he now presses for more easy and transient pleasures; the longer he lives, the further he must walk to cut wood (since he has planted no trees on his estate). Wastoure suggests the king should send them to live separately, for the day is drawing to a close, and he cannot bear to see his opponent any longer.

*Lines 456–503: The King's Judgement*

In response to Wastoure's request, the king sends Wynnere to the papal court and Wastoure to London. In the future, they must be kept apart, and the king seems to have in mind a continuous programme of alternation between the two. Wynnere is sent to Rome, to live in luxury for which he does not have to pay, on the condition that he will return to follow the king to war and to finance his campaigns. Wastoure's activities seem also to be commended but redirected, as his instructions are to encourage commerce and consumption in the city, where merchants and workers will reap the profit, as Wastoure himself had argued earlier. Accordingly, Wastoure's activities will support the followers of Wynnere, who in turn will aid the king.

The manuscript breaks off before the conclusion of the king's speech, and while it seems unlikely there is much missing from the text, the king has been unable to offer more than a narrowly practical and temporary solution to the ethical problems raised by the debate. Given the complexity of the issues and the ambivalence of the king's summing-up, we must regret all the more the historical accident that has removed the final comments of the authoritative narrative voice with which the poem opened.

## CRITICAL STUDIES

The history of the early reception of *Wynnere and Wastoure* is dominated by textual studies concerned to establish the date and provenance of the poem, and its relationship to other alliterative poems of the period, especially *Piers Plowman* and *The Parlement of the Thre Ages*. Such preoccupations are not unusual in the scholarship of the late nineteenth and early twentieth centuries, but the influence of these developments on modern studies of medieval literature is rarely acknowledged. The criticism of alliterative poetry, for example, continually appeals to notions of literary history and poetic influence, a critical canon and evaluative criteria that were established by the first editors and commentators. Interestingly, there seems to be little relation between recent criticism of *Wynnere and Wastoure* and other alliterative poems and current politicizing or historicist reassessments of more popular writers such as Chaucer and, to a lesser extent, Langland. One reason for this might be the fact that alliterative verse has been consistently treated as a poetic corpus distinguished by its metre;

and as a result, literary and metrical or stylistic history remain the
major areas of discussion. Accounts of *Wynnere and Wastoure* are
chiefly concerned to place or frame the poem in a particular literary
context (which in turn often determines interpretation): for example,
in a tradition of debate poetry, of satirical critique, or more commonly,
in the metrical context of the fourteenth-century alliterative revival.
Rather surprisingly, for a work that is generally considered to be at
least ambitious and innovative, and at best, of considerable poetic
power, *Wynnere and Wastoure* has received comparatively little interpretative attention of a specific nature. We may suspect that had the
poem been complete, or had attempts to establish common authorship with *The Parlement of the Thre Ages* been more successful, then the
temptation to discover a new alliterative master would have kept the
poem rather more in favour.

As far as *Wynnere and Wastoure*'s relation with the alliterative revival
is concerned, the presumed early date of the poem and its comparatively late discovery have given it the status of a kind of 'missing link' in
many accounts of the revival. Various assumptions about the stylistic
development of alliterative poetry are drawn from the poet's
undoubted confidence with his metre and with formulæ and colloca-
tions that appear elsewhere in the alliterative corpus. The poet is
working within a well-established poetic, so the argument goes, and
we may safely assume that examples of earlier, more tentative alliterative composition have been lost. Scholars are naturally rather
cautious about postulating a date for this interest in re-formulating or
reconstructing the long alliterative line without rhyme and yet are less
reluctant to trace lines of influence from those works which do survive.[1] John Burrow describes *Piers Plowman* as a reaction against the
excesses of the high alliterative style and vocabulary represented by
*Wynnere and Wastoure*, considered inappropriate for a London audience in whom Langland could presume less familiarity with the alliterative style.[2] This argument has been very influential in the stylistic and
aesthetic assessment of these two poems, and the traditions they
represent. *Wynnere and Wastoure* occupies a central place in Derek
Pearsall's account of alliterative poetry, standing as it does at the
beginning of the 'movement', and sharing stylistic aspects and
thematic concerns of the two schools into which Pearsall divides the

[1] Turville-Petre, for example, dates *Joseph of Arimathie* before 1349 on stylistic evidence, in *The Alliterative Revival*, p. 24.

[2] J. A. Burrow, 'The Audience of *Piers Plowman*', *Anglia*, lxxv (1957), 373–84.

poetry of the revival: first, the *Piers Plowman* group, or 'the political, didactic and complaint tradition'; and second, the *Gawain* group, of historical epics, the poems in the *Gawain* manuscript, *The Parlement of The Thre Ages* and *St Erkenwald*. 'If I call it a showpiece,' he writes, 'this is not meant to suggest that it is a deliberate advertisement of the potential of alliterative verse, but that this, judging from its known and presumed influence in both branches of alliterative poetry, may well have been how it struck contemporary writers.'[1]

Space does not permit a more detailed examination of this aspect of the poem's history, and its relationship with *Piers Plowman*, but these classifications of alliterative poetry according to style and subject-matter, and indeed, the persistent grouping of alliterative poetry into a separate corpus deserve further interrogation. Blake has argued against this categorization, but Lawton writes of a 'temper' shared by alliterative poets which finds its inspiration in *Piers Plowman*, and Langland's concern with 'penance and the role of vernacular writing in inducing it'.[2] As far as *Wynnere and Wastoure* is concerned, readings governed by this desire for a coherent literary history or, indeed, to recuperate the poem for a particular critical method are more frequent than detailed readings of the poem itself.

In 1950, John Speirs published a two-part series of 'revaluings' of medieval poetry in *Scrutiny* (later reprinted in *Medieval English Poetry*) invoking many of the characteristic Leavisite preoccupations about the organic English society of the past, and the robustness or vigour of the individual poet as claims on our attention.[3] He argues, for example, that the debate in *Wynnere and Wastoure* is a form of primitive ritual flyting; and that the poet owes less to the dream poetry of medieval France than native English or even Scandinavian tradition. He is concerned to link Winner and Waster respectively with Medill Elde and Ʒouthe in *The Parlement of the Thre Ages*, as indeed, are many commentators, but stresses that these oppositions represent the seasonal alternation of summer and winter. According to Speirs, the *Wynnere and Wastoure* poet is chiefly concerned with economics, implicitly arguing that spending and saving are both necessary to a healthy economy, and that the king's task is to balance the claims of both ways.

[1] *Old English and Middle English Poetry*, p. 160.

[2] See Blake's critique of Turville-Petre's *The Alliterative Revival* in *Review*, i (1979), 205–14; and Lawton, 'The Unity of Middle English Alliterative Poetry', p. 74.

[3] '*Wynnere and Wastoure* and *The Parlement of the Thre Ages*', *Scrutiny*, xvii (1950), 221–52.

Jerry D. James finds irony and ambiguity as the determining features of the poem: his essay, published in 1964, is the first attempt to apply the New Critical practice of close reading to the poem.[1] Unfortunately, many of his readings are blind to medieval conventions and poetic traditions. For example, he suggests the herald is presented in an unfavourable light when he must arm himself without assistance, while this is fitting behaviour for a hero in the ethos of traditional epic. He finds barbed satirical attacks on Edward III and the Black Prince (for he accepts Gollancz's identification of these figures), and makes an important distinction between Wynnere and Wastoure, arguing that Wastoure's arguments are the more sophisticated and indeed, that the narrator tends to favour Wastoure in his presentation and characterization of the debate.

Bestul's *Satire and Allegory in Wynnere and Wastoure* remains the only monograph on the poem, and is invaluable for its survey of past scholarship, and Bestul's research into the intellectual background of the poem and the means by which this background was disseminated into fourteenth-century English culture. His work does much to counter Gollancz's view of the poem as a hastily written piece, inspired solely by contemporary conditions, but Bestul is still concerned to read the poem as a debate which relies heavily on topical satire to make its point. He offers a rather sophisticated argument to account for the perceived deficiencies in the debate itself, suggesting that the audience would have recognized the many argumentative fallacies propounded by Wynnere and Wastoure, and have condemned each accordingly as representatives of the extremes of avarice and prodigality.

Bestul's recognition of the Aristotelian scheme of the poem has been very influential on subsequent criticism of the poem, and finds interesting fruit in the discussion by David Starkey, who considers the poem as part of his larger discussion of the household as an institution of economic and political power in the later middle ages.[2] Starkey considers various literary and iconographic representations of the household, emphasizing the two main divisions of the royal household—the lord chamberlain's department and the lord steward's department—and their claims to the respective courtly virtues of magnificence and providence. Aristotelian magnanimity consists in

---

[1] 'The Undercutting of Conventions in *Wynnere and Wastoure*', *MLQ* xxv (1964), 243–58.

[2] 'The Age of the Household: Politics, Society and the Arts, c. 1350–c. 1550', in *The Later Middle Ages*, ed. S. Medcalf (London, 1981), pp. 225–90, esp. 253–8.

reconciling these virtues, and Starkey's discussion places Wynnere and Wastoure's debate before their king firmly in this context, probably the most challenging reading of the poem and its relationship to its social context.[1]

Two further articles have appeared more recently. Nicolas Jacobs argues that the poem belongs to the 'balanced or resolved type' of debate, yet traces elements in the debate and the prologue that suggest the poet's sympathies lie with Wastoure.[2] He suggests that through Wastoure, the poet is 'idealising an old-fashioned, essentially feudal and rural social order as a *distributive* society ... as against what he sees as the undesirable new development of an *acquisitive*, essentially mercantile and urban society'.[3] Jacobs is far less confident than earlier critics of the poet's abilities and control over his material. David Harrington, on the other hand, stresses the poet's interest in indeterminacy in debate and in creating an unreliable narrator.[4] Following Bestul, Harrington contends that each disputant's speech would have been received more critically by the audience of the poem than by his opponent or the king, and concludes that 'a poet succeeds if he stimulates us to respond more intelligently than his characters do'.[5]

From this survey of representative criticism, it is clear that the poem's critical history can be divided fairly evenly into two movements: an old style historicism concerned to determine the political, intellectual and stylistic contexts of the poem, and a formalist criticism that pays little heed to the poem's undoubted interest in the disparity between ethical theory and economic practice.

It might be argued, for example, that the poet is chiefly concerned to explore the connotations of the words winning and wasting in the changing social and economic contexts of the later middle ages. Traditionally, winning is the positive and wasting the negative term, but the poem challenges this hierarchy by making Wastoure in some ways the more attractive character, and by exploring the resonances of these two terms. Wasting, then, can mean prodigality and luxury, but it can also mean the natural and grateful consumption of agricultural

---

[1] See also R. H. Hilton, *The English Peasantry in the Later Middle Ages* (Oxford, 1975), for a brief discussion of the poet's implicit criticism of both Wynnere and Wastoure's failure to re-invest capital, pp. 177–8.

[2] 'The Typology of Debate and the Interpretation of *Wynnere and Wastoure*', *RES* n.s. xxxvi (1985), 481–500.

[3] Jacobs, p. 498.

[4] 'Indeterminacy in *Winner and Waster* and *The Parliament of the Three Ages*', *Chaucer Review*, xx (1986), 246–57.

[5] Harrington, p. 256.

produce as gifts from God, or the household expenses necessary to maintain a lord's honour. Winning can certainly still be the prudent acquisition of provisions and money, but the poet does seem impatient with the tendency to be concerned only with profit. If Wynnere is portrayed as a merchant, a member of an increasingly powerful class in the fourteenth century, then the poem can be regarded as an attempt to wrestle with the ethical implications of this profession, and the social and political ambitions of the middle classes, particularly in London. The proliferation in this period of sumptuary laws designed to enforce visible distinctions between classes testifies to contemporary anxiety about the inadequacy of traditional hierarchies and estates theory to account for the ready access to wealth and political power enjoyed by some members of the middle classes. The poet is also critical of Wastoure, however, and he can perhaps be identified, as we will see, with those disaffected members of the aristocracy who developed different networks of power in the form of political and military allegiances which cut across and neglected traditional family lines. Either way, the poem seems concerned about change, and while Jacobs is right to find traces of authorial nostalgia, the poem is also characterized by its shifting narrative focus and unstable perspective, and its imaginative engagement in the task of fleshing out a traditional ethical opposition in contemporary social terms.

Given that we lack the narrator's conclusion, it is not possible to be sure that this is intended as a resolved or an indeterminate debate. The poet's interest is captured by different aspects and arguments in turn, and he is quite inconsistent, for example, in his treatment of the two armies. They are not only described at vastly different length, but we are told that they are all strangers to England and ignorant of its laws. Then, once attention shifts to the two knights who kneel together before the king as members of his household, the two armies are forgotten as the king addresses his servants in distinctly domestic and familiar terms. As Wynnere and Wastoure introduce themselves formally, the allegorical aspect of the debate seems to come to the fore, but as soon as they begin to characterize themselves and each other, it becomes much more difficult to see Wynnere in particular as one of the *knyghtis full comely*. The poet has chosen not to present him iconographically as avarice, even though some of Wastoure's criticisms underline this identification. The king's judgement, as I have suggested above, completely ignores the ethical or social dimensions of the debate and resorts to a time-serving practical solution to the

enmity of the two figures. Their constant refrain is that each is sufficient for the kingdom, and that they cannot be reconciled (though
Wastoure does claim that Wynnere needs him). The king takes them
at their word and decides to separate them. This unsatisfactory deci-
sion, which solves neither the economic nor the ethical problems
raised in the debate, seems ironically to reflect the degree to which the
two anonymous knights have been dramatically realized as individual
figures, even personalities. The poet cannot collapse them back into
unproblematic allegorical abstractions, and the king cannot resolve
their dispute in ethical terms that might guide his own practices. His
concern is in financing his wars and rewarding his followers. We
might conclude that the poet is unable to maintain a clear distinction
between the literal and the allegorical modes.

But perhaps this very distinction will need to be probed further in
future readings. The poet's perception of disparities between current
economic and social conditions and traditional ideologies should also
be considered in more detail. Langland's treatment of Wasters will be
important in any such discussion, and I have tried to indicate some
possible lines of inquiry in the Commentary.

## EDITORIAL PRINCIPLES

### Editorial History

Israel Gollancz published the first text of *Wynnere and Wastoure* in 1897
as an Appendix to his edition of *The Parlement of the Thre Ages*. He
made a few corrections to passages that were obviously corrupt, but
the transcription from the manuscript was imperfect, and it was not
until 1920 that Gollancz produced a complete edition. Perceiving that
the text was deficient in many places, he confidently regularized many
aspects of the poem's metre, alliteration and grammar, occasionally
also adjusting its sense and subject matter, making over 130 changes to
the text and completing deficient lines affected by damage to the
manuscript. He offered a fairly full commentary, glossary, and a
modernized version of the poem, but no statement of editorial principles. His introduction has been highly influential in subsequent
views of the poem as a hastily written, orally transmitted topical satire
on the economic policies of Edward III and the Black Prince (see sec-
tion on Date above), while most of his changes to grammar, metre and
alliteration are governed by a very strict understanding of the rules of

alliterative composition and Middle English syntax. For example, most b-verses are emended to provide a two-syllable 'dip' between stresses, while tense, person, and number are almost always brought into strict agreement.

This edition received mixed reviews. J. R. Hulbert, J. M. Steadman, and D. Everett criticized the extent of Gollancz's re-writing of the text and in particular his insistence that the poem demonstrate such a regular rhythm.[1] A number of mistakes in transcription were corrected by Steadman, but few of these corrections were incorporated into the second edition of 1931, which was seen through the press by Dr M. Day. In spite of these critical reservations, Gollancz's text did find favour with several commentators who advocated the restoration of regular and full alliteration in other texts, and while Holthausen and Kölbing defended several manuscript readings rejected by Gollancz, they were also keen to propose alternative emendations at other points, incorporating words and phrases used in other alliterative poems.[2]

Several anthologized versions of the poem were published in the 1950s and 1960s by Rolf Kaiser, Ann Haskell, and Francis Berry, and the poem was the subject of two dissertations by Karen Stern and Lon Mark Rosenfield.[3] John Burrow and Thorlac Turville-Petre have also published anthologized versions of the text, but Gollancz's influence on all editions (with the exception of Turville-Petre's very conservative text) is great, and his edition of 1920 has remained the standard edition, being reprinted in 1974.

While the fact that the poem exists in only one manuscript might encourage editorial conservatism in a new edition, there is no doubt that the text is corrupt in many places. And while a diplomatic text might seem attractive, especially where a heavily emended edition has been so influential, Turville-Petre's very conservative text is readily available. The present text, then, is offered as an hypothetical reconstruction of a good fifteenth-century text of the poem: certainly, Thornton's manuscript is geographically and chronologically too distanced from the original for the complete recovery of the poem's

---

[1] J. R. Hulbert, *MP* xviii (1921), 499–503; J. M. Steadman, Jr., *MLN* xxxvi (1921), 103–10; D. Everett, *RES* ix (1933), 213–18.

[2] F. Holthausen, *Beiblatt zur Anglia*, xxxiv (1923), 14–16; A. Brandl, *Archiv*, cxlix (1926), 287–8. F. Kölbing had reviewed the text of 1897 in *ESt* xxv–xxvi (1898), 273–89, while Holthausen considered the second edition in *Beiblatt zur Anglia*, xliv (1933), 173–4.

[3] K. M. Stern, 'A Critical Edition of *Winner and Waster*' (M.Phil., London, 1973); L. M. Rosenfield, '*Wynnere and Wastoure*: A Critical Edition' (Ph.D., Columbia, 1975).

original forms to be within our grasp. Yet as contemporary manuscript studies show, there is much we can learn from medieval scribal habits and practices, and I have tried to record as many features of the manuscript as possible in the apparatus beneath the text, and in the commentary.[1]

Inevitably, several unsatisfactory readings remain, usually in places which indicate that Thornton or a previous copyist was trying to make sense of a corrupt exemplar, and where the original reading remains obscure. The Commentary draws attention to such passages. I have rarely attempted to correct the syntax of the text to provide grammatical agreement and consistency of tense or even person, though number is sometimes corrected. Our limited knowledge of Middle English syntax commends caution in this area, while the syntax of *Wynnere and Wastoure* often seems paratactic rather than hypotactic. At the same time it is also characteristically knotty and dense, which makes judgements about syntax very difficult. I have tried to keep emendation of such passages to a minimum.

Recent developments in editorial theory remind us how difficult it is to preserve an absolutely consistent editorial practice, and that textual criticism is inevitably predicated on prior assumptions and expectations of the author's style and competence. No edition can lay claim to absolute authority, the perfect recovery of the original text. When a text survives in only one manuscript, the situation is even more extreme, since any editorial divergence from the copy-text is conjectural and inescapably the result of subjective judgement. By the same token, however, if *Wynnere and Wastoure* is to be read as anything more than an incomplete palaeographical curiosity, it is necessary to conjecture about original forms. In arguing as cogently as possible for each emendation or conjecture, by clearly marking the signs of his or her passing, the editor can at least draw attention to the process of textual reconstruction. Any edition must be regarded as provisional, an act of interpretation or contextualization. The genre of the edition, its characteristic narrative stance, its decorum and its form are objects of study pending investigation in their own right: in the meantime, we are probably right to approach the editorial task with suspicion.

---

[1] Transcriptions from the manuscript are also available in unpublished form: Rainbow (1960), Stern (1973), and S. Trigg, '*Wynnere and Wastoure*: A Critical Reconstruction with Commentary' (Ph.D., Melbourne, 1984).

*Corrections to the Text*

All emendations to the manuscript are discussed in the Commentary, but they are classified here for convenience.

A. *Mechanical error.* (1) Omission of word: 372, 409, 445, 454, 484, 492. (2) Misreading of abbreviations, letter forms, omissions of letter(s), word division: 15, 64 (twice), 83, 125, 127, 157, 164, 166, 190, 201 (twice), 264, 270, 288, 317, 336, 337, 364, 390, 395, 408, 411, 420, 434, 476, 502. (3) Anticipation or catching: 58, 91, 94, 136, 144, 177, 189, 300, 400.

B. *Scribal substitution.* (1) Unconscious: 121, 176/186, 369. (2) Deliberate: 79, 236, 266, 314, 321, 494.

C. *Completion of damaged text.* 353, 354, 355, 356, 357, 358, 359, 468, 469, 470, 471, 472, 473, 485, 500.

*Note on the Text*

The text was transcribed from Additional Manuscript 31042 in the British Library, and checked against a microfilm of that manuscript. This microfilm was made by the Library in April 1969, before the manuscript was repaired and re-bound in 1972. Some new readings are now possible, and the Commentary draws attention to these, but the subsequent deterioration of the manuscript has obscured several readings. The final letters of *swannes* 340, *folowe* 395, *pore* 420, and -*add*- of *laddes* 375 are badly faded. The final leaf has been torn and repaired through *one* 430, *ben* 470, *passe* 476, *morow* 478, *spr(e)* 485, and *egh(e)* 487, and these readings have been confirmed from the microfilm.

The text employs a number of contractions and abbreviations, only a few of which present any difficulty for transcription. Chief among these is the curved, straight, or hooked line which appears over many words. It is interpreted as indicating the absence of a nasal consonant in *lūbardye* and *connÿges*, for example, and the doubling of a nasal consonant after a short vowel in *woñe*, *blÿñes*, *Wÿñere*, and *soñe* 'sun'. In several words such as *ratoūs*, *woūdirs*, this sign appears over minim strokes which could represent *n*, but on the strength of *grounde* and *graunte*, these words are expanded as *ratouns*, *woundirs*. In *soñe* 'son', *toñg* and *cōmes*, the stroke is clearly redundant. The usual abbreviations for *with*, *and*, *þou*, *þat*, *er*, *re*, *ar*, *ra*, *ur*, *sir*, *es*, and *ett* also appear, although with more frequency on the last leaf. It is assumed that the stroke through -*ll*, *h*, and the turned-up flourish after final *n* or *m* are ornamental and do not signify the omission of final *-e*. The following abbreviations have been expanded silently in accordance with the scribe's normal spelling habits: 7 (*and*); þt (*þat*), wᵗ (*with*); þᵘ (*þou*).

Thornton does not distinguish between *I* and *J*, and often uses *y* for *þ*: these letters have been transcribed according to their phonetic value. *V* is used consistently for initial *u*, and is retained in this position. Double *f* is used for capital *F*, but the capital of many letters such as *a*, *c*, *s*, and *w* is differentiated only by size, and it is often impossible to judge if a *littera notabilior* is intended in the middle of a line, where capitals of other letters appear. The text, however, follows modern conventions of capitalization and those of the *MED* for word division. Emendations are enclosed within square brackets and the apparatus records rejected manuscript readings and features of the manuscript, especially Thornton's own corrections to his text. Punctuation has been kept to a minimum, to avoid imposing a complex hypotactic system upon a looser syntactic model. There is no punctuation in the manuscript, and I have used modern conventions to elucidate the text where confusion might arise. The mid-line break is indicated with a small space (even though, unlike many medieval copyists, Thornton does not indicate this pause) and the reader is reminded of the rhythmical function of this break and the frequency with which lines are end-stopped. Illuminated initials are marked in bold type, and the poem is also divided into fitts, which, again, are not marked in the manuscript.

# SELECT BIBLIOGRAPHY

The listing in the Bibliography is chronological within each category.

## EDITIONS

Gollancz, Israel (ed.), *The Parlement of the Thre Ages*, with *Wynnere and Wastoure* as an Appendix (London, 1897).

Gollancz, Israel (ed.), *A Good Short Debate Between Winner and Waster: An Alliterative Poem on Social and Economic Problems in England in the Year 1352, with Modern English Rendering*. Select Early English Poems, 3 (London, 1920, rpt. Cambridge, 1974); 2nd edn. rev. M. Day (London, 1930, rpt. New York, 1981).

Stern, Karen, 'A Critical Edition of *Winner and Waster*' (M.Phil., London, 1973).

Rosenfield, Lon Mark, '*Wynnere and Wastoure*: A Critical Edition' (Ph.D., Columbia, 1975).

Trigg, Stephanie, '*Wynnere and Wastoure*: A Critical Reconstruction with Commentary' (Ph.D., Melbourne, 1984).

## ANTHOLOGIZED VERSIONS

R. Kaiser (ed.), *Middle English* (West Berlin, 1958, rev. 1961).

F. Berry (ed.), 'An Anthology of Middle English Poetry', in *The Age of Chaucer*, ed. B. Ford, *Pelican Guide to English Literature*, vol. I (Harmondsworth, 1959).

A. S. Haskell (ed.), *A Middle English Anthology* (Garden City, New York, 1969).

J. A. Burrow (ed.), *English Verse 1300–1500* (London, 1977).

T. Turville-Petre (ed.), 'An Anthology of Medieval Poems and Drama', in *Medieval Literature: Chaucer and the Alliterative Tradition*, ed. B. Ford, *New Pelican Guide to English Literature*, vol. I, pt. 1 (Harmondsworth, 1982).

## TRANSLATION

Gardner, John, *The Alliterative Morte Arthure, The Owl and the Nightingale, and Five Other Middle English Poems in Modernized Versions* (Carbondale, 1971).

## THE MANUSCRIPT

Brunner, K., 'Hs. Brit. Mus. Additional 31042', *Archiv*, cxxxii (1914), 316–27.

Stern, K. M., 'The London Thornton Miscellany: A New Description of BM Addit. MS. 31042', *Scriptorium*, xxx (1976), 26–37, 201–18.

Keiser, George R., 'Lincoln Cathedral Library MS. 91: Life and Milieu of the Scribe', *SB* xxxii (1979), 158–79.

Horrall, Sarah M., 'The London Thornton Manuscript: A New Collation', *Manuscripta*, xxiii (1979), 99–103.

Horrall, Sarah M., 'The Watermarks on the Thornton Manuscripts', *N&Q* n.s. xvii (1980), 385–6.

Keiser, George R., 'More Light on the Life and Milieu of Robert Thornton', *SB* xxxvi (1983), 111–19.

Hamel, Mary, 'Scribal Self-Corrections in the Thornton *Morte Arthure*', *SB* xxxvi (1983), 119–37.

Hanna, Ralph III, 'The London Thornton Manuscript: A Corrected Collation', *SB* xxxvii (1984), 122–30.

Hanna, Ralph III, 'The Growth of Robert Thornton's Books', *SB* xl (1987), 51–61.

## TEXT

Kölbing, F., Review of *The Parlement of the Thre Ages*, ed. I. Gollancz (1897), *ESt* xxv–xxvi (1898), 273–89.

Hulbert, J. R., Review of *Wynnere and Wastoure*, ed. I. Gollancz (1920), *MP* xviii (1921), 499–503.

Steadman, J. M., Review of *Wynnere and Wastoure*, ed. I. Gollancz (1920), *MLN* xxxvi (1921), 103–10.

Holthausen, F., Review of *Wynnere and Wastoure*, ed. I. Gollancz (1920), *Beiblatt zur Anglia*, xxxiv (1923), 14–16.

Steadman, J. M., 'Notes on *Wynnere and Wastoure*', *MLN* xxxviii (1923), 310–11.

Brandl, A., Review of *Wynnere and Wastoure*, ed. I. Gollancz (1920), *Archiv*, cxlix (1926), 287–8.

Holthausen, F., Review of *Wynnere and Wastoure*, ed. I. Gollancz (1931), *Beiblatt zur Anglia*, xliv (1933), 173–4.

Everett, Dorothy, Review of *Wynnere and Wastoure*, ed. I. Gollancz (1932), *RES* ix (1933), 213–18.

Turville-Petre, Thorlac, 'The Prologue of *Wynnere and Wastoure*', *LeedsSE* n.s. xviii (1987), 19–29.

## LANGUAGE

Serjeantson, M. S., 'The Dialects of the West Midlands in Middle English', *RES* iii (1927), 54–67, 186–203, 219–31.

Offord, M. Y., ed. *The Parlement of the Thre Ages*, EETS 246 (1959).

Rainbow, R. S., 'A Linguistic Study of *Wynnere and Wastoure* and *The Parlement of the Thre Ages*' (Ph.D., Chicago, 1960).

## DATE, AUTHORSHIP, AND PROVENANCE

Neilson, George, 'A Note on *Wynnere and Wastoure*', *The Athenaeum*, 3 Aug., cxviii (1901), 157.

Gollancz, Israel, 'A Note on *Wynnere and Wastoure*', *The Athenaeum*, 24 Aug., cxviii (1901), 254–5.

Neilson, George, 'A Note on *Wynnere and Wastoure*', *The Athenaeum*, 7 Sept., cxviii (1901), 319.

Gollancz, Israel, 'A Note on *Wynnere and Wastoure*', *The Athenaeum*, 14 Sept., cxviii (1901), 351.

Bradley, Henry, '*Wynnere and Wastoure*', *The Athenaeum*, 18 April, cxxi (1903), 498–9.

Neilson, George, '*Wynnere and Wastoure*', *The Athenaeum*, 16 May, cxxi (1903), 626–7.

Bradley, Henry, '*Wynnere and Wastoure*', *The Athenaeum*, 23 May, cxxi (1903), 657–8.

Bradley, Henry, '*Wynnere and Wastoure*', *The Athenaeum*, 27 June, cxxi (1903), 816–7.

Gollancz, Israel, 'Ich dien', Letters to the *Times Literary Supplement*, 1, 8, and 22 Aug., 1918.

Neilson, George, '*Wynnere and Wastoure* and the *Awntyrs*', *The Athenaeum*, 13 June, cxxi (1903), 754–5.

Neilson, George, '*Wynnere and Wastoure*', *The Athenaeum*, 15 Aug., cxxii (1903), 220–1.

Hulbert, J. R., 'The Problems of Authorship and Date of *Wynnere and Wastoure*', *MP* xviii (1920), 31–40.

Steadman, J. M., 'The Date of *Wynnere and Wastoure*', *MP* xix (1921), 211–19.

Steadman, J. M., 'The Authorship of *Wynnere and Wastoure* and *The Parlement of the Thre Ages*: A Study in Methods of Determining the Common Authorship of Middle English Poems', *MP* xxi (1923), 7–13.

Anderson, J. M., 'A Note on the Date of *Wynnere and Wastoure*', *MLN* xliii (1928), 47–9.

Gollancz, Israel, Note on the Frontispiece to *Chivalry: A Series of Studies to Illustrate its Historical Significance and Civilizing Influence*, ed. E. Prestage (London, 1928).

Oakden, J. P., 'A Note on the Unity of Authorship of *Wynnere and Wastoure* and *The Parlement of the Thre Ages*', *RES* x (1934), 200–2.

Stillwell, Gardiner, '*Wynnere and Wastoure* and the Hundred Years' War', *ELH* viii (1941), 241–7.

McColly, William B., 'The Audience of *The Parlement of the Thre Ages* and *Wynnere and Wastoure*' (Ph.D., UCLA, 1957).

Moran, Dennis V., '*Wynnere and Wastoure*: An Extended Footnote', *NM* lxxiii (1972), 683–5.

Lawton, David A., 'Literary History and Scholarly Fancy: The Date of Two Middle English Alliterative Poems', *Parergon*, xviii (1977), 17–25.

Salter, Elizabeth, 'The Timeliness of *Wynnere and Wastoure*', *MÆ* xlvii (1978), 40–65.

Bennett, Michael J., *Community, Class and Careerism: Cheshire and Lancashire Society in the Age of Sir Gawain and the Green Knight* (Cambridge, 1983).

Havely, N. R., 'The Dominicans and Their Banner in *Wynnere and Wastoure*', *N&Q* n.s. xxx (1983), 207–9.

Trigg, Stephanie, 'Israel Gollancz's *Wynnere and Wastoure*: Political Satire or Editorial Politics?', in *Medieval English Religious and Ethical Literature: Essays in Honour of G. H. Russell*, ed. Gregory Kratzmann and James Simpson (Cambridge, 1986), pp. 115–27.

## GENERAL STUDIES

Putnam, Bertha, *The Place in Legal History of Sir William Shareshull* (Cambridge, 1950).

Speirs, J., '*Wynnere and Wastoure* and *The Parlement of the Thre Ages*', *Scrutiny*, xvii (1950), 241–9 (rpt. in *Medieval English Poetry: The Non-Chaucerian Tradition* [London, 1957]).

James, Jerry D., 'The Undercutting of Conventions in *Wynnere and Wastoure*', *MLQ* xxv (1964), 243–58.

Silverstein, T., '*Sir Gawain*, Dear Brutus and Britain's Fortunate Founding: A Study in Comedy and Convention', *MP* lxii (1964), 189–206.

Hieatt, Constance, '*Wynnere and Wastoure* and *The Parlement of the Thre Ages*', *AN&Q* iv (1966), 100–14.

Oiji, Takero, 'An Essay on *Wynnere and Wastoure*, with Special Reference to the Political, Economic and Religious Attitudes of the Poet', *Studies in English Literature* (Tokyo), xliii (1966), 1–14, 127–8.

Elliott, R. W. V., 'The Topography of *Wynnere and Wastoure*', *ES* xlviii (1967), 134–40.

Bellamy, J. G., *The Law of Treason in England in the Later Middle Ages* (Cambridge, 1970).

Bellamy, J. G., *Crime and Public Order in England in the Later Middle Ages* (London, 1973).

Bestul, T. H., *Satire and Allegory in Wynnere and Wastoure* (Lincoln, Nebraska, 1974).

Newton, Stella M., *Fashion in the Age of the Black Prince: A Study of the Years 1340– 65* (Woodbridge, 1980).

Coleman, Janet, *Medieval Readers and Writers* (London, 1981).

Starkey, David, 'The Age of the Household: Politics, Society and the Arts, c.1350–c.1550', in *The Later Middle Ages*, ed. S. Medcalf (London, 1981).

Jacobs, Nicolas, 'The Typology of Debate and the Interpretation of *Wynnere and Wastoure*', *RES* n.s. xxxvi (1985), 481–500.

Harrington, David V., 'Indeterminacy in *Winner and Waster* and *The Parliament of the Three Ages*', *Chaucer Review*, xx (1986), 246–57.

Brown, Peter and Andrew Butcher, 'Teaching "Crisis, Text and Image"', *Literature and History*, xiii (1987), 3–13.


## *WYNNERE AND WASTOURE* AND THE ALLITERATIVE REVIVAL

Everett, Dorothy, *Essays on Middle English Literature*, ed. P. M. Kean (Oxford, 1955).

Burrow, J. A., 'The Audience of *Piers Plowman*', *Anglia*, lxxv (1957), 373–84.

Hussey, S. S., 'Langland's Reading of Alliterative Poetry', *MLR* lx (1965), 163–70.

Salter, Elizabeth, 'The Alliterative Revival', *MP* lxiv (1966), 146–50, 233–37.

Williams, D. J., 'Alliterative Poetry in the Fourteenth and Fifteenth Centuries', in *The Middle Ages*, ed. W. F. Bolton (London, 1970).

Pearsall, D. A., *Old English and Middle English Poetry* (London, 1977).

Turville-Petre, Thorlac, *The Alliterative Revival* (Cambridge, 1977).

Salter, Elizabeth, 'Alliterative Modes and Affiliations in the Fourteenth Century', *NM* lxxix (1978), 25–35.

Pearsall, D. A., 'The Origins of the Alliterative Revival', in *The Alliterative Tradition in the Fourteenth Century*, ed. B. S. Levy and P. E. Szarmach (Kent, Ohio, 1981).

Lawton, David A. (ed.), *Middle English Alliterative Poetry and its Literary Background* (Cambridge, 1982).

Lawton, David A., 'The Unity of Middle English Alliterative Poetry', *Speculum*, lviii (1983), 72–94.

# WYNNERE AND WASTOURE

Here begynnes a tretys and god schorte refreyte bytwixe Wynnere and
Wastoure.

**S**ythen that Bretayne was biggede    and Bruyttus it aughte
Thurgh the takynge of Troye    with tresone withinn
There hathe selcouthes bene sene    in seere kynges tymes
Bot neu*er* so many as nowe    by the nyne dele.
For nowe alle es witt and wyles    that we with delyn,
Wyse wordes and slee    and icheon wryeth othere.
Dare neu*er* no westren wy    while this werlde lasteth
Send his sone southewarde    to see ne to here
That he ne schall holden byhynde    when he hore eldes.
Forthi sayde was a sawe    of Salomon the wyse,    10
It hyeghte harde appone honde,    hope I no no*þ*er,
When wawes waxen schall wilde    and walles bene doun
And hares appon herthe-stones    schall hurcle in hire fourme
And eke boyes of blode    with boste and with pryde
Schall wedde ladyes in londe    and lede h[em] at will,    15
Thene dredfull domesdaye    it draweth neghe aftir.
Bot whoso sadly will see    and the sothe telle
Say it newely will neghe    or es neghe here.
Whylome were lordes in londe    *þ*at loued in thaire hertis
To here makers of myrthes    *þ*at matirs couthe fynde    20
And now es no frenchipe in fere    bot fayntnesse of hert,
Wyse wordes withinn    *þ*at wroghte were neu*er*
Ne redde in no romance    *þ*at eu*er* renke herde.
Bot now a childe appon chere    withowtten chyn-wedys
*þ*at neu*er* wroghte thurgh witt    thies wordes togedire    25
Fro he can jangle als a jaye    and japes telle
He schall be lenede and louede    and lett of a while
Wele more *þ*an *þe* man    that made it hymseluen.
Bot neu*er* *þe* lattere at the laste    when ledys bene knawen;
Werke wittnesse will bere    who wirche kane beste.    30
**B**ot I schall tell ȝow a tale    *þ*at me bytyde ones,
Als I went in the weste    wandrynge myn one.
Bi a bonke of a bourne    bryghte was the son*n*e,

15 hem] hir        16 neghe] *after* one hande *cancelled*

Vndir a worthiliche wodde   by a wale medewe
Fele floures gan folde   ther my fote steppede.      35
I layde myn hede one ane hill   ane hawthorne besyde
The throstills full throly   they threpen togedire
Hipped vp heghwalles   fro heselis tyll othire
Bernacles with thayre billes   one barkes þay roungen
þe jay janglede one heghe,   jarmede the foles,      40
þe bourne full bremly rane   þe bankes bytwene.
So ruyde were þe roughe stremys   and raughten so heghe
That it was neghande nyghte   or I nappe myghte
For dyn of the depe watir   and dadillyng of fewllys.
Bot as I laye at the laste   þan lowked myn eghne      45
And I was swythe in a sweuen   sweped belyue.
f. 177ᵛ  Me thoghte I was in the werlde,   I ne wiste in whate ende,
One a loueliche lande   þat was ylike grene
þat laye loken by a lawe   the lengthe of a myle.
In aythere holte was ane here   in hawberkes full brighte,      50
Harde hattes appon hedes   and helmys with crestys;
Brayden owte thaire baners   bown for to mete;
Schowen owte of the schawes   in schiltrons þay felle
And bot the lengthe of a launde   thies lordes bytwene.
And alle prayed for the pese   till the prynce come      55
For he was worthiere in witt   than any wy ells
For to ridde and to rede   and to rewlyn the wrothe
That aythere here appon h[eth]e   had vntill othere.
At the creste of a clyffe   a caban was rerede
Alle raylede with rede   the rofe and the sydes      60
With Ynglysse besantes full brighte   betyn of golde
And ichone gayly vmbygone   with garters of inde
And iche a gartare of golde   gerede full riche.
Then were th[er] wordes in þe webbe   werped of he[u],
Payntted of plunket   and poyntes bytwene      65
þat were fourmed full fayre   appon fresche lettres
And alle was it one sawe   appon Ynglysse tonge,
'Hethyng haue the hathell   þat any harme thynkes,
Now the kyng of this kythe   kepe hym oure lorde!'
Vpon heghe one the holt   ane hathell vp stondes      70
Wroghte als a wodwyse   alle in wrethyn lokkes

38 tyll] y *written over* o      50 full] *after* attyrede *cancelled*      58 hethe] hate
64 ther] thre   heu] he

With ane helme one his hede    ane hatte appon lofte
And one heghe one þe hatte    ane hattfull beste,
A lighte lebarde and a longe    lokande full kene
Ʒarked alle of ʒalowe golde    in full ʒape wyse.        75
Bot that þat hillede the helme    byhynde in the nekke
Was casten full clenly    in quarters foure;
Two with flowres of Fraunse    before and behynde
And two out of Ynglonde    with [orfraied] bestes,
Thre leberdes one lofte    and thre on lowe vndir.       80
At iche a cornere a knoppe    of full clene perle
Tasselde of tuly silke    tuttynge out fayre.
And by þe cabane I knewe    the k[nyght]e that I see
And thoghte to wiete or I went    wondres ynewe.
And als I waytted withinn    I was warre sone       85
Of a comliche kynge    crowned with golde
Sett one a silken bynche    with septure in honde,
One of the louelyeste ledis    whoso loueth hym in hert
That euer segge vnder sonn    sawe with his eghne.
This kynge was comliche clade    in kirtill and mantill,       90
Bery-brown was [the bleaunt]    brouderde with fewlys,       f. 178ʳ
Fawkons of fyne golde    flakerande with wynges
And ichone bare in ble    blewe als me thoghte
A grete gartare of ynde    [gerede full riche].
Full gayly was that grete lorde    girde in the myddis       95
A brighte belte of ble    broudirde with fewles
With drakes and with dukkes    daderande þam semede
For ferdnes of fawkons fete    lesse fawked þay were.
And euer I sayd to myselfe,    'full selly me thynke
Bot if this renke to the reuere    ryde vmbestounde.'       100
The kyng biddith a beryn    by hym þat stondeth
One of the ferlyeste frekes    þat faylede hym neuer,
'Thynke I dubbede the knyghte    with dynttis to dele
Wende wightly thy waye    my willes to kythe
Go bidd þou ʒondere bolde batell    þat one þe bent houes       105
That they neuer neghe    nerre togedirs
For if thay strike one stroke    stynte þay ne thynken.'
'Ʒis lorde,' said þe lede,    'while my life dures.'

79 orfraied] sex grym     83 knyghte] kynge     91 the bleaunt] his berde
brouderde] b *written over* d     94 gerede full riche] girde in the myddes (g *written over* d)

He dothe hym doun one þe bonke   and dwellys a while  
Whils he busked and bown was   one his beste wyse.        110  
He laped his legges in yren   to the lawe bones  
With pysayne and with pawnce   polischede full clene  
With brases of broun stele   brauden full thikke  
With plates buklede at þe bakke   þe body to ȝeme  
With a jupown full juste   joynede by the sydes,        115  
A brod chechun at þe bakke,   þe breste had anoþer,  
Thre wynges inwith   wroghte in the kynde  
Vmbygon with a gold wyre.   When I þat gome knewe  
What! he was ȝongeste of ȝeris   and ȝapeste of witt  
þat any wy in this werlde   wiste of his age.        120  
He brake a braunche in his hande   and [brayde] it swythe,  
Trynes one a grete trotte   and takes his waye  
There bothe thies ferdes folke   in the felde houes,  
**Sayd,** 'loo! the kyng of this kyth   þer kepe hym oure lorde  
Send[es] erande by me   als hym beste lyketh        125  
That no beryn be so bolde   one bothe his two eghne  
Ones to strike one stroke   n[e] stirre none nerre  
To lede rowte in his rewme   so ryall to thynke,  
Pertly with ȝoure powers   his pese to disturbe.  
For this es the vsage here   and euer schall worthe        130  
f. 178ᵛ  If any beryn be so bolde   with banere for to ryde  
Withinn þe kyngdome riche   bot the kynge one  
That he schall losse the londe   and his lyfe aftir.  
Bot sen ȝe knowe noghte this kythe   ne the kynge ryche  
He will forgiffe ȝow this gilt   of his grace one.        135  
Full wyde hafe I walked   [thies wyes amonges]  
Bot sawe I neuer siche a syghte,   segge, with myn eghne  
For here es alle þe folke of Fraunce   ferdede besyde  
Of Lorreyne, of Lumbardye   and of Lawe Spayne,  
Wyes of Westwale   þat in were duellen,        140  
Of Ynglonde, of Yrlonde,   Estirlynges full many  
þat are stuffede in stele   strokes to dele.  
And ȝondere ʽa banerʼ of blake   þat one þe bent houes  
With thre bulles of ble white   brouden withinn  
And iche one hase of henppe   hynged a corde        145

121 brayde] caughten     125 Sendes] Send his     127 ne] no     136 thies wyes amonges] amonges thies wyes one     143 a baner] *in margin, position indicated by caret marks*     144 bulles] bibulles

Seled with a sade lede,   I say als me thynkes;
That hede es of holy kirke   I hope he be there
Alle ferse to the fighte   with the folke þat he ledis.
Anoþer banere es vpbrayde   with a bende of grene
With thre hedis white-herede   with howes one lofte,                    150
Croked full craftyly   and kembid in the nekke.
Thies are ledis of this londe   þat schold oure lawes ʒeme
That thynken to dele this daye   with dynttis full many.
I holde hym bot a fole þat fightis   whils flyttynge may helpe
When he hase founden his frende   þat fayled hym neuer.                 155
The thirde banere one bent   es of blee whitte
With sexe gale[g]s, I see,   of sable withinn
And iche one has a brown brase   with bokels twayne.
Thies are Sayn Franceys folke   þat sayen alle schall fey worthe.
They aren so ferse and so fresche   þay feghtyn bot seldom.            160
I wote wele for wynnynge   thay wentten fro home,
His purse weghethe full wele   that wanne thaym all hedire.
The fourte banere one the bent   was brayde appon lofte
With bothe the brerdes of blake,   a bal[l]e in the myddes
Reghte siche as the sonne es   in the someris tyde                    165
When it hase moste of þe may[n]e   one Missomer euen.
That was Domynyke this daye   with dynttis to dele,
With many a blesenande beryn   his banere es stuffede,
And sythen the pope es so priste   thies prechours to helpe
And Fraunceys with his folke   es forced besyde                       170
And alle the ledis of the lande   ledith thurgh witt
There es no man appon molde   to machen þaym agayne
Ne gete no grace appon grounde   vndir God hymseluen.                 f. 179ʳ
And ʒitt es the fyfte appon þe felde   þe faireste of þam alle,
A brighte banere of blee whitte   with three bore hedis.              175
Be any crafte þat I kan   Carmes thaym semyde
For þay are the [ledis] þat louen   oure lady to serue.
If I scholde say þe sothe   it semys no nothire
Bot þat the freris with othere folke   shall þe felde wynn.
The sexte es of sendell   and so are þay alle,                        180
Whitte als the whalles bone   whoso the sothe tellys
With beltys of blake   bocled togedir,

---

157 galegs] galeys     164 balle] balke     166 mayne] maye     176 Be any
crafte . . . semyde] *copied after* 185     177 ledis] ordire     179 shall] h *written over*
al     181 whalles] h *written over* a

The poyntes pared off rownde,    þe pendant awaye
And alle the lethire appon lofte    þat one lowe hengeth
Schynethe alle for scharpynynge    of the schauynge iren.          185
The ordire of þe Austyns    for oughte þat I wene,
For by the blussche of the belte    the banere I knewe.
And other synes I seghe    sett appon lofte,
Some wittnesse of wolle    and some of wyne tounnes,
Some of merchandes merke[s]    so many and so thikke          190
That I ne wote in my witt    for alle this werlde riche
Whatt segge vnder the sonne    can the sowme rekken.
And sekere one þat other syde    are sadde men of armes,
Bolde sqwyeres of blode,    bowmen many,
þat if thay strike one stroke    stynt þay ne thynken          195
Till owthir here appon hethe    be hewen to dethe.
Forthi I bid ȝow bothe    that thaym hedir broghte
That ȝe wend with me    are any wrake falle
To oure comely kyng    that this kythe owethe,
And fro he wiete wittirly    where þe wronge ristyth          200
Thare nowthir wye be wrothe    to wirche als he d[em]eth.'
Off ayther rowte ther rode owte    a renke als me thoghte,
Knyghtis full comly    one coursers attyred
And sayden, 'Sir sandisman    sele the betyde!
Wele knowe we the kyng,    he clothes vs bothe          205
And hase vs fosterde and fedde    this fyve and twenty wyntere.
Now fare þou byfore    and we schall folowe aftire.'
And now are þaire brydells vpbrayde    and bown one þaire wayes,
Thay lighten doun at þe launde    and leued thaire stedis,
Kayren vp at the clyffe    and one knees fallyn.          210
The kynge henttis by þe handes    and hetys þam to ryse
And sayde, 'welcomes, heres, as hyne    of oure house bothen.'
The kynge waytted one wyde    and the wyne askes,
Beryns broghte it anone    in bolles of siluere.
Me thoghte I sowpped so sadly    it sowrede bothe myn eghne          215
And he þat wilnes of this werke    to wete any forthire
Full freschely and faste    for here a fitt endes.

f. 179ᵛ  **B**ot than kerpede the kynge, sayd,    'kythe what ȝe hatten
And whi the hates aren so hote    ȝoure hertis bytwene

184 hengeth] *after* hey *cancelled*          186 The ordire ... I wene] *copied after* 175
189 Some] Some of          190 merkes] merke          195 thynken] *after* blyn *cancelled*
201 wye] wyes    demeth] doeth

If I schall deme ȝow this day    dothe me to here.'    220
'Now certys lorde,' sayde þat one,    'the sothe for to telle,
I hatt Wynnere, a wy    that alle this werlde helpis
For I lordes cane lere    thurgh ledyng of witt.
Thoo þat spedfully will spare    and spende not to grete,
Lyve appon littill-whattes    I lufe hym the bettir.    225
Witt wiendes me with    and wysses me faire,
Aye when gadir my gudes    than glades myn hert
Bot this felle false thefe    þat byfore ȝowe standes
Thynkes to strike or he styntt    and stroye me for euer.
Alle þat I wynn thurgh witt    he wastes thurgh pryde,    230
I gedir, I glene    and he lattys goo sone,
I pryke and I pryne    and he the purse opynes.
Why hase this cayteffe no care    how men corne sellen?
His londes liggen alle ley,    his lomes aren solde,
Downn bene his dowfehowses,    drye bene his poles.    235
The deuyll wounder the wele    he weldys at home
Bot hungere and heghe howses    and howndes full kene.
Safe a sparthe and a spere    sparrede in ane hyrne,
A bronde at his bede-hede    biddes he no noþer
Bot a cuttede capill    to cayre with to his frendes.    240
Then will he boste with his brande    and braundesche hym ofte,
This wikkede weryed thefe    that Wastoure men calles,
That if he life may longe    this lande will he stroye.
Forthi deme vs this daye    for Drightyns loue in heuen
To fighte furthe with oure folke    to owthire fey worthe.'    245
'Ȝee Wynnere,' quod Wastoure,    'thi wordes are hye
Bot I schall tell the a tale    that tene schall the better
When thou haste waltered and went    and wakede alle þe nyghte,
And iche a wy in this werlde    that wonnes the abowte,
And hase werpede thy wyde howses    full of wolle sakkes,    250
The bemys benden at the rofe,    siche bakone there hynges,
Stuffed are sterlynges    vndere stelen bowndes.
What scholde worthe of that wele    if no waste come?
Some rote, some ruste    some ratouns fede.
Let be thy cramynge of thi kystes    for Cristis lufe of heuen,    255
Late the peple and the pore    hafe parte of thi siluere,
For if thou wydwhare scholde walke    and waytten the sothe

---

224 spare] *after* spende *cancelled*    236 wounder] wounder one

Thou scholdeste reme for rewthe     in siche ryfe bene the pore.
For and thou lengare thus lyfe,     leue thou no noþer,
Thou schall be hanged in helle     for that thou here spareste.          260
For siche a synn haste þou solde     thi soule into helle
f. 180ʳ And there es euer wellande woo     worlde withowtten ende.'
'Late be thi worde, Wastoure,'     quod Wynnere the riche,
'Thou melleste of a mater     tho[u] madiste it thiseluen.
With thi sturte and thy stryffe     thou stroyeste vp my gudes          265
In [waytt]inge and in wakynge     in wynttres nyghttis,
In owttrage, in vnthrifte     in angarte pryde.
There es no wele in this werlde     to wasschen thyn handes
That ne es gyffen and grounden     are þou it getyn haue.
Thou ledis renkes in thy rowte     wele ry[c]hely attyrede,          270
Some hafe girdills of golde     þat more gude coste
Than alle þe faire fre londe     that ȝe byfore haden.
Ȝe folowe noghte ȝoure fadirs     þat fosterde ȝow alle
A kynde herueste to cache     and cornes to wynn
For þe colde wyntter and þe kene     with gleterand frostes          275
Sythen dropeles drye     in the dede monethe.
And thou wolle to the tauerne     byfore þe tonne-hede
Iche beryne redy with a bolle     to blerren thyn eghne
Hete the whatte thou haue schalte     and whatt thyn hert lykes
Wyfe, wedowe or wenche     þat wonnes there aboute.          280
Then es there bott "fille in" and "feche forthe"     florence to schewe
"Wee hee" and "worthe vp"     wordes ynewe.
Bot when this wele es awaye     the wyne moste be payede fore.
Than lympis ȝowe weddis to laye     or ȝoure londe selle,
For siche wikked werkes     wery the oure lorde.          285
And forthi God laughte that he louede     and leuede þat oþer
Iche freke one felde     ogh þe ferdere be to wirche.
Teche thy men for to tille     and ty[n]en thyn feldes,
Rayse vp thi renthowses,     ryme vp thi ȝerdes
Owthere hafe as þou haste done     and hope aftir werse          290
þat es firste þe faylynge of fode     and than the fire aftir
To brene the alle at a birre     for thi bale dedis.
The more colde es to come     als me a clerke tolde.'
'Ȝee Wynnere,' quod Wastoure,     'thi wordes are vayne,
With oure festes and oure fare     we feden the pore.          295

264 thou] tho          266 wayttinge] playinge          270 rychely] ryhely
274 cache] *after* caste *cancelled*          288 tynen] tymen

It es plesynge to the prynce    þat paradyse wroghte,
When Cristes peple hath parte    hym payes alle the better
Then here ben hodirde and hidde    and happede in cofers
That it no sonn may see    thurgh seuen wyntter ones,
Owthir freres it feche    when thou fey worthes                    300
To payntten with thaire pelers    or pergett with thaire walles.
Thi sone and thi sektours    ichone slees othere,
Maken dale aftir thi daye    for thou durste neuer,
Mawngery ne myndale    ne neuer myrthe louediste.
A dale aftir thi daye    dose the no mare                         305
þan a lighte lanterne    late appone nyghte
When it es borne at thi bakke,    beryn, be my trouthe.          f. 180ᵛ
Now wolde God that it were    als I wisse couthe
That thou Wynnere, thou wriche    and Wanhope thi brothir
And eke ymbryne dayes    and euenes of sayntes,                   310
The Frydaye and his fere    one the ferrere syde
Were drownede in the depe see    there neuer droghte come,
And dedly synn for thayre dede    were endityde with twelue,
And thies beryns one the bynches    with [bonets] one lofte
That bene knowen and kydde    for clerkes of the beste,          315
Als gude als Arestotle    or Austyn the wyse,
That alle schent were those schalkes    and Scharshull itwiste
þat saide I prikkede with powere    his pese to distourbe.
Forthi, comely kynge    that oure case heris,
Late vs swythe with oure swerdes    swyngen togedirs             320
For nowe I `se´ it es full sothe    þat sayde es full ȝore
"The richere of ranke wele    the rathere will drede,
The more hauande þat he hathe    the more of hert feble".'
Bot than this wrechede Wynnere    full wrothely he lukes,
Sayse, 'þis es spedles speche    to speken thies wordes.         325
Loo! this wrechide Wastoure    that wydewhare es knawenn.
Ne es nothir kaysser ne kynge    ne knyghte þat the folowes,
Barone ne bachelere    ne beryn that thou loueste
Bot foure felawes or fyve    that the fayth owthe.
And he schall dighte thaym to dyne    with dayntethes so many    330
þat iche a wy in this werlde    may wepyn for sorowe.
The bores hede schall be broghte    with plontes appon lofte
Buktayles full brode    in brothes there besyde

300 freres] it freres         314 bonets] howes        317 itwiste] it wiste
321 se] se es (se *in margin,* es *above caret mark after* I)

Venyson with the frumentee    and fesanttes full riche
Baken mete therby    one the burde sett                                    335
Chewettes of choppede flesche    charbi[na]de fewlis
And iche a segge þat I see    has sexe mens do[l]e.
If this were nedles note    anothir comes aftir,
Roste with the riche sewes    and the ryalle spyces
Kiddes clouen by þe rigge,    quarterd swannes,                           340
Tartes of ten ynche    þat tenys myn hert
To see þe borde ouerbrade    with blasande disches
Als it were a rayled rode    with rynges and stones.
The thirde mese to me    were meruelle to rekken
For alle es Martynmesse mete    þat I with moste dele,                    345
Noghte bot worttes with the flesche    withowt wilde fowle
Saue ane hene to hym    that the howse owethe.
And he will hafe birdes bownn    one a broche riche
Barnakes and buturs    and many billed snyppes
Larkes and lyngwhittes    lapped in sogoure                               350
Wodcokkes and wodwales    full wellande hote
Teeles and titmoyses    to take what hym lykes

f. 181ʳ,    [Caud]ils of connynges    and custadis swete
col. 1    [Dario]ls and dische-metis    þat ful dere coste
[Maw]mene þat men clepen    ȝour mawes to fill,                           355
[Ich]e a mese at a merke    bytwen twa men
[þat s]othe bot brynneth for bale    ȝour bowells within.
[Me t]enyth at ȝour trompers,    þay tounen so heghe
[þat ic]he a gome in þe gate    goullyng may here.
þen wil þay say to þamselfe    as þay samen ryden,                        360
Ȝe hafe no myster of the helpe    of þe heuen kyng.
þus are ȝe scorned by skyll    and schathed þeraftir
þat rechen for a repaste    a rawnsom of siluer.
Bot one[s] I herd in a haule    of a herdmans tong,
"Better were meles many    þan a mery nyghte".'                           365
And he þat wilnes of þis werke    for to wete forthe
Full freschely and faste    for here a fit endes.

336 charbinade] charbiande        337 dole] doke        348 birdes] *after* bown *cancelled*        353 Caudils] *defective to* -ils        connynges] g *damaged by worm hole*        354 Dariols] *defective to* -oils        355 Mawmene] *defective to* -mene        356 Iche] *defective to* -e        357 þat sothe] *defective to* -othe        358 Me tenyth] *defective to* -enyth        359 þat iche] *defective to* -he        364 ones] one

'ȝee Wynnere,' quod Wastour,   'I wote wele myseluen
What sall lympe of þe, lede,   within [lit]e ȝeris.
Thurgh þe poure plenté of corne   þat þe peple sowes    370
þat God will graunte of his grace   to growe on þe erthe
Ay to appaire þe pris   and [it] passe nott to hye,
Schal make þe to waxe wod   for wanhope in erthe
To hope aftir an harde ȝere   to honge þiseluen.
Woldeste þou hafe lordis to lyfe   as laddes on fote,    375
Prelates als prestes   þat þe parischen ȝemes,
Prowde marchandes of pris   as pedders in towne?
Late lordes lyfe als þam liste,   laddes as þam falles
þay þe bacon and beefe,   þay botours and swannes
þay þe roughe of þe rye,   þay þe rede whete    380
þay þe grewell gray   and þay þe gude sewes
And þen may þe peple hafe parte   in pouert þat standes,
Sum gud morsell of mete   to mend with þair chere.
If fewlis flye schold forthe   and fongen be neuer
And wild bestis in þe wodde   wonne al þaire lyue    385
And fisches flete in þe flode   and ichone ete oþer
Ane henne at ane halpeny   by halfe ȝeris ende;
Schold not a ladde be in londe   a lorde for to serue.
þis wate þou full wele   witterly þiseluen,
Whoso wele schal wyn   a wastour 'mo[st]e' he fynde    390
For if it greues one gome   it gladdes anoþer.'
Now quod Wynner to Wastour,   'me wondirs in hert
Of thies poure penyles men   þat peloure will by,
Sadills of sendale   with sercles full riche.    f. 181ʳ, col. 2
Lesse [þat] ȝe wrethe ȝour wifes   þaire willes to folowe    395
Ȝe sellyn wodd aftir wodde   in a wale tyme,
Bothe þe oke and þe assche   and alle þat þer growes.
þe spyres and þe ȝonge sprynge   ȝe spare to ȝour children
And sayne God wil graunt it his grace   to grow at þe last
For to [schadewe] ȝour sones   bot þe schame es ȝour ownn,    400
Nedeles saue ȝe þe soyle   for sell it ȝe thynken.
Ȝour forfadirs were fayne   when any frende come
For to schake to þe schawe   and schewe hym þe estres
In iche 'holt' þat þay had   ane hare for to fynde,

368 seluen] *written above the line*     369 lite] fewe     372 it] *om.*
390 moste] moþe *(in margin, position indicated by caret marks)*     395 þat] and
400 schadewe] saue to     404 holt] *in right-hand margin, position indicated by caret marks*

Bry*n*g to the brod lau*n*de　　bukkes ynewe　　　　　　　405
To lache and to late goo　　to lightten þaire hertis.
Now es it sett and solde　　my sorowe es þe more,
Waste[d] alle wilfully　　ȝo*ur* wyfes to paye.
That are had [ben] lordes i*n* londe　　and ladyes riche
Now are þay nysottes of þe new gett　　so nysely attyred　　410
With [sy]de slabbande sleues　　sleght to þe grou*n*de
Ourlede all vmbto*ur*ne　　with ermyn aboute
þat es as harde, as I hope,　　to handil i*n* þe derne
Als a cely symple wenche　　þat neu*er* silke wroghte.
Bot whoso lukes on hir lyre,　　oure lady of heuen,　　　　415
How scho fled for ferd　　ferre out of hir kythe
Appon ane amblande asse　　withowtte*n* more p*ri*de
Safe a barne i*n* hir barme　　and a broken heltre
þat Joseph held i*n* hys hande　　þat hend for to ȝeme.
All þofe scho walt al þis werlde　　hir w[e]des wer pore　　420
For to gyf ensa*m*ple of siche　　for to schewe oþ*er*
For to leue pompe and p*ri*de,　　þat pou*er*te ofte schewes.'
**Than** þe Wasto*ur* wrothly　　cast*es* vp his eghne
And said, 'þou Wyn*n*ere, þou wriche,　　me wou*n*dirs i*n* h*er*t
What hafe oure clothes coste þe,　　caytef, to by　　　　425
þat þou schal birdes vpbrayd　　of þaire bright wedis,
Sythe*n* þat we vouchesafe　　þat þe siluer payen.
It lyes wele for a lede　　his lem*m*an to fynde,
Aftir hir faire chere　　to forthir hir herte.
Then will scho loue hy*m* lelely　　as hir lyfe one　　　　430
Make hy*m* bolde and bown　　with brandes to smytte
f. 181ᵛ,　To schonn schenchipe and schame　　þ*er* schalkes ere gadird.
col. 1　And if my peple be*n* prode　　me payes alle þe bett*er*
To [s]ee þam faire and free　　tofore with myn eghne.
And ȝe negardes appon nyghte　　ȝe nappen so harde,　　435
Routten at ȝo*ur* raxilly*n*g,　　raysen ȝo*ur* hurdes.
Ȝe beden wayte one þe wedir　　þe*n* wery ȝe þe while
þat ȝe nade hightilde vp ȝo*ur* houses　　and ȝo*ur* hyne raysed.
Forthi, Wyn*n*ere, with wronge　　þou wastes þi tyme
For gode day ne glade　　getys þou neu*er*.　　　　　　440
þe deuyll at þi dede-day　　schal delyn þi gudis,

---

408 Wasted] Wastes　　　409 ben] *om.*　　　411 syde] elde　　　419 hys] h
*written over* a　　　420 wedes] wordes　　　430 hir] ir *damaged by worm hole*
434 see] fee

þo þou woldest þat it were    wyn þay it neuer,
þi skathill sectours    schal seuer þam aboute
And þou hafe helle full hotte    for þat þou here saued,
þou tast [no] tent one a tale    þat tolde was full ȝore.          445
I hold hym madde þat mournes    his make for to wyn,
Hent hir þat hir haf schal    and hold hir his while.
Take þe coppe as it comes,    þe case as it falles,
For whoso lyfe may lengeste    lympes to feche
Woodd þat he waste schall    to warmen his helys          450
Ferrere þan his fadir dide    by fyvetene myle.
Now kan I carpe no more    bot Sir Kyng, by þi trouthe,
Deme vs where we duell schall,    me thynke þe day hyes.
ȝit harde sore es myn [hert]    and harmes me more
Euer to see in my syghte    þat I in soule hate.'          455
The kynge louely lokes    on þe ledis twayne,
Says, 'blynnes, beryns, of ȝour brethe    and of ȝoure brode worde
And I schal deme ȝow this day    where ȝe duelle schall,
Aythere lede in a lond    þer he es loued moste.
Wende, Wynnere, þi waye    ouer þe wale stremys,          460
Passe forthe by Paris    to þe pope of Rome,
þe cardynalls ken þe wele,    will kepe þe ful faire
And make þi sydes in silken    schetys to lygge
And fede þe and foster þe    and forthir thyn hert
As leefe to worthen wode    as þe to wrethe ones.          465
Bot loke, lede, be þi lyfe,    when I lettres sende
þat þou hy þe to me home    on horse or one fote,
And when I knowe þou will co[me]    he schall cayre vttire          f. 181ᵛ,
And lenge with anoþer lede    til þou þi lefe [take].          col. 2
For þofe þou bide in þis burgh    to þi ber[yinge-daye]          470
With hym happyns þe neuer    a fote for [to holde].
And thou, Wastoure, I will    þat þou wonn[e scholde]
þer moste waste es of wele    and wyng [þer vntill].
Chese þe forthe into þe chepe,    a chambre þou rere,
Loke þi wyndowe be wyde    and wayte þe aboute          475
Where any p[eti]t beryn    þurgh þe burgh passe.
Teche hym to þe tauerne    till he tayte worthe,

---

445 no] *om.*        454 hert] *om.*        468 come] *defective from* co-        469 take]
*defective*        470 beryinge-daye] *defective from* ber-        471 to holde] *defective*
472 wonne scholde] *defective from* wonn-        473 wyng þer vntill] *defective from* wyng
(*see Commentary*)        476 petit] potet

Doo hy*m* drynke al ny3te    þat he dry be at morow,
Sythe*n* ken hy*m* to þe crete    to co*m*forth his vaynes,
Bry*n*ge hy*m* to Bred Strete,    bikken þi fynger,                    480
Schew hy*m* of fatt chepe    scholdirs ynewe,
"Hotte for þe hungry"    a hen o*þer* twayne.
Sett hy*m* softe one a sege    and sythe*n* send aft*er*
[And] bry*n*g out of þe burgh    þe best þou may fynde
And luke thi knafe hafe a knoke    bot he þe clothe spre[de].        485
Bot late hym paye or he passe    and pik hy*m* so clene
þat fynd a peny i*n* his purse    and put owte his eghe.
When þat es dro*n*ken and don    duell þ*er* no leng*er*
Bot teche hy*m* owt of the townn    to trotte aftir more
Then passe to þe pultrie,    þe peple þe knowes                       490
And ken wele þi kato*ur*    to knawen þi fode,
The herou*n*s, þe hastelete3    þe henne wele [to] s*er*ue
þe p*er*trikes, þe plou*er*s    þe o*þer* pulled byrddes
þe albus, þ[e end]es    þe egretes dere,
þe more þou wastis þi wele    þe bett*er* þe Wyn*n*er lykes.          495
And wayte to me, þou Wyn*n*ere,    if þou wilt wele chefe,
When I wende appon werre    my wyes to lede
For at þe proude pales    of Parys þe riche
I thynk to do it i*n* ded    and dub þe to knyghte
And giff giftes full grete    of golde and of sil[uer]               500
To ledis of my legyance    þat lufen me i*n* h*er*t.
And sythe*n* [k]ayre as I come    with knyght*es* þat me foloen
To þe kirke of Colayne    þ*er* þe kynges ligges. . . .'

---

484 And] *om.*        485 sprede] *defective from* spr-        492 to] *om.*
494 þe endes] þis oþer foules        500 siluer] *defective from* sil-        502 kayre]
layren

# COMMENTARY

The Commentary discusses all emendations made to the text, analyses difficult words and phrases and attempts to elucidate some of the historical and legal references in the poem. I have not aimed at a comprehensive coverage of the poem's literary background or context, for there are no obvious sources for the poem except perhaps *Piers Plowman*. The best account of the intellectual tradition of the poem is found in Thomas Bestul's *Satire and Allegory in Wynnere and Wastoure* (Lincoln, Nebraska, 1974).

Most alternative conjectures and readings are discussed here, though other editions are mentioned only where their readings differ from Gollancz's. Many of the editions or reviews cited in the commentary are referred to by name of the editor or author, such as Gollancz, Stern, Burrow, Turville-Petre, Steadman, Schumacher, Holthausen, and Kölbing: see the Select Bibliography for details. Several other works are referred to by author's name. These are:

R. W. V. Elliott, 'The Topography of *Wynnere and Wastoure*', *ES* xlviii (1967), 134–40.

S. M. Newton, *Fashion in the Age of the Black Prince: A Study of the Years 1340–65*. Woodbridge, Suffolk, 1980.

E. Salter, 'The Timeliness of *Wynnere and Wastoure*', *MÆ* xlvii (1978), 40–65.

The titles of alliterative poems refer to the following editions:

*Sir Gawain and the Green Knight*, ed. J. R. R. Tolkien and E. V. Gordon. 2nd edn. rev. N. Davis. Oxford, 1967.

Langland, *Piers Plowman: The A Version*, ed. G. Kane. London, 1960.

Langland, *Piers Plowman: The B Version*, ed. G. Kane and E. T. Donaldson. London, 1975.

*Piers Plowman by William Langland: An Edition of the C-Text*, ed. D. Pearsall. London, 1978.

*The Parlement of the Thre Ages*, ed. M. Y. Offord. EETS, 246 (1959).

Dictionaries consulted are abbreviated in the following manner.

*AND*    *Anglo-Norman Dictionary*.

Clark Hall and Meritt.   *A Concise Anglo-Saxon Dictionary*.

*DOST*   *Dictionary of the Older Scottish Tongue*.

*EDD*   *English Dialect Dictionary*.

Godefroy.   *Dictionnaire de l'ancien français*.

*MED*   *Middle English Dictionary*.

*OED*   *Oxford English Dictionary*.

*Incipit.* The poem is categorized here as a formal, rhetorical exercise—a *tretys and god schorte refreyte*—whose subject is the opposition between Wynnere and Wastoure. We cannot identify the author of this *incipit*, but it is clear that in grouping the poem with *The Parlement of the Thre Ages*, Thornton considered it primarily an ethical work.

1–2. The poet alludes briefly to the tradition of Britain's founding by Brutus, the great-grandson of Aeneas, a legend drawn from Geoffrey of Monmouth's *Historia Regum Britanniae* and used as an opening motif in a number of alliterative poems (cf. *Sir Gawain and the Green Knight* 13–15 and see also D. Pearsall, *Old English and Middle English Poetry* (London, 1977), p. 158). The theme is given a new twist here, as the poet appeals to Britain's violent origins to account for her present unhappy state.

5. **witt and wyles:** 'cunning and trickery'. Gollancz alters the phrase to *witt and wylle*, citing a similar passage in *Thomas of Erceldoune's Prophecy*, but the common medieval dichotomy of 'wit' and 'will' would be inappropriate here. *Wyles* and *witt* are personified in *Piers Plowman* C. IV. 77–8.

6. **icheon wryeth othere:** The subject of this phrase is *wyse wordes and slee*: *wryeth* derives from OE *wrēon* 'cover' and we may thus translate, 'Cunning and knowing words, each one obscuring the sense of the next'. The same grammatical construction is used at lines 302 and 386.

9. **holden byhynde:** 'remain at home'. Gollancz can produce no evidence for his gloss 'fare badly, be badly off', though this sense is adopted by *MED holden* v. (1), 24 (a). The line depends on a shift in syntax of the kind we come to expect in the poem, the first *he* referring to the son, and the second to the father in his old age, 'So he won't remain at home when he grows old and grey'.

15. **hem:** *Ladyes* requires an accusative plural pronoun after *leden* and the manuscript's *hir* is corrected to *hem*. Gollancz reads *lede [at hir] will*, but *leden* 'marry' normally requires a direct object. *Hir* was probably caught from *hire* in line 13, while these unusual West Midlands pronominal forms were possibly inherited with the 'prophecies' of lines 12–16 from an older apocalyptic tradition. Cf. 'Thomas of Erceldoune's Prophecy' in *Historical Poems of the Fourteenth and Fifteenth Centuries*, ed. R. H. Robbins (New York, 1959), p. 28.

19–23. Gollancz places an emended version of line 21 (*And now es no frenchipe [o]n fere bot fayntnesse of hert*) after line 6; though the lines make good sense as they stand, and can be construed as follows: 'Once there were lords in the land who delighted in their hearts to listen to writers of diversions who knew how to express serious matters. But now there is no friendliness where men are gathered (*no frenchipe in fere*); only cowardice and weakness of spirit, wise counsels spoken inwardly (*withinn*) but never expressed (*wroghte*) nor read in any narrative heard by any man.' The poet is less concerned in this prologue about declining interest in oral poetry, as Gollancz (who emends *wroghte* in line 22 to *writen*) would have it, than to establish his narrative voice as that of an authoritative, prophetic truth-teller who *sadly will see and the sothe telle* (line 17).

Burrow suggests that *fynde(n) matir(s)* might have been a recognized translation of 'inventio' ('The Audience of *Piers Plowman*', *Anglia*, lxxv (1957), p. 382).

24–30. The poet's abuse of other more popular entertainers is a familiar medieval topos, found in works as diverse as *Deor*, *Piers Plowman*, the Chandos Herald's *Life of the Black Prince*, and Froissart's *Chroniques*. M. Gsteiger traces its origins to the *Rhetorica ad Herennium* ('Note sur les préambules des chansons de geste', *Cahiers de Civilisation Médiévale*, ii (1959), p. 219).

27. **lenede:** All editors have read *leuede* 'believed' from the manuscript, but *lenede* is the more likely reading, with the sense 'listened to, attended to', or even 'given permission, allowed (to read)' or 'rewarded'. See *MED lenen* v. (1), from OE *hlinian* (Merc. *hleonian*) and *lenen* v. (3), from OE *lǣnan*.

36. **hill:** This form may represent OE *hyll* or the less common *huyle* as in *Pearl* 41, where it means 'cluster of plants, a mound overgrown with plants'. This is recorded as a modern form in East Lancashire (see Elliott, p. 135).

**hawthorne:** The archetypal spring blossom in medieval English poetry, the hawthorn tree is also associated with the supernatural world: the dreamers in *Death and Liffe* and Henryson's *Lion and the Mouse* also fall asleep under a hawthorn tree.

39. **Bernacles with thayre billes one barkes þay roungen:** Like the hawthorn tree, the barnacle geese are indications of the marvellous nature of the meadow in which the dreamer falls asleep. Accounts of their fabled manner of reproduction appear in Giraldus Cambrensis' *Topographia Hibernia* and Mandeville's *Travels*: they were popularly thought to grow in shells which adhered to branches of trees overhanging water. See also T. H. White, *The Book of Beasts: The Translation of a Twelfth-Century Latin Bestiary* (New York, 1960), pp. 267–8.

**one barkes þay roungen:** Gollancz reads *barkes* as the plural 'barks' of trees, on which the birds 'rang' with their beaks. But *barkes* can also be 'shells of nuts', while *roungen* is best read as a present plural form of *MED roungen*, from OF *ro(u)ngier* 'gnaw, champ'.

40. **jarmede the foles:** Both *jarmede* and *foles* are obscure here, although *foles* is probably a deliberate scribal substitution by a previous scribe for the name of another, unfamiliar bird since the word is elsewhere spelled *fewllys*. *MED* relates *jarmede* to *chirmen* 'chirp' without explaining the changes to initial consonant and vowel. *Jarmede* may be an altered form of ON *jarma* 'bleat', or *jarmr* 'bleating', found in *sauði-jarmr* 'bleating of sheep' and *fugls-jarmr* 'bleating, crying of birds'. This word would be related to OE *geomor*, MnE *yammer*, but the initial sound may have been voiced under the influence of OF *gemir*, *giembre*, from Latin *gemere*: the confident alliteration with *jay* and *janglede* suggests the poet is using a familiar word.

**44. dadillyng:** a rare, presumably imitative word. *EDD* records a number of similar and related words meaning 'chattering, gossiping, tattling' but also 'waddling (of ducks), staggering'. We also find *daderande* at line 97, which plainly means 'trembling, shivering'. *Dadillyng* can best be glossed as 'commotion, tumult', describing the chirping and the restless movement of the birds.

**49. loken by a lawe:** 'enclosed by earthworks'. The *lawe* that encircles the clearing is an artificial mound of the kind thrown up around the playing space or *lande* of the medieval theatre. Elliott argues convincingly that the dream-setting here also draws on earlier forms of pageantry and the more dramatic aspects of the tournament: the *caban* of line 59, for example, is likened to the judge's box or pavilion at a tournament (Elliott, p. 139). The scene also recalls the *fair feeld ful of folk* in *Piers Plowman*; for other analogues and the suggestion that the poet may have known Huon de Mery's *Li Tornoimenz Antecrit* see Bestul, pp. 36–9.

The two armies under leaders whose banners are described by a herald are elements drawn from the *mêlée*, or mock battle, while the prayer for peace and the drinking of wine may reflect the religious observances and revelry which accompanied duels. The intensity of hatred and threats of mortal injury also suggest parallels with the duel, sometimes used as a legal means of settling a dispute which could not be resolved in court (cf. lines 154–5) and was a fight to the death in the presence of the king or his deputy. As in the tournament, the king acted as judge. Cf. G. A. Lester, 'Chaucer's Knight and the Medieval Tournament', *Neophilologus*, lxvi (1982), 460–8.

**55. And alle prayed for the pese:** Kölbing described the prayer for peace as unintelligible, since the two armies were keen to be allowed to destroy each other, and Gollancz emended the line in 1920 to read *And als I prayed....* The prayer, however, seems an important part of the dramatic, ritualized framing of the debate.

**58. hethe:** The manuscript reads *That aythere here appon hate had vntill othere* and must be corrupt; the copyist may have anticipated the initial letters of *had.* Kölbing proposed the reading *hethe* 'battlefield' on the strength of line 196 *Till owthir here appon hethe be hewen to dethe.*

**64. Then were ther wordes:** Gollancz corrects the manuscript's *thre wordes* to *th[ies] wordes*, but the reading adopted here provides a less emphatic, more gradual introduction of the Garter motto in line 68. The error may have been caused by the expansion of an abbreviation as *re* instead of *er.*

**werped of heu:** 'woven in colour'. Manuscript *he* has generally been accepted as a variant of *heghe* 'high', though the motto is not cast up on a banner, but woven in minute detail into the blue cloth of which the garters are made (see *OED Warp v.* III, 20a, c), and indeed, the spelling *he* for *heghe* would be unique in the poem (see Glossary). *Werped of he* may obscure a form of *MED heu* n. 'colour, paint, die', describing the motto as 'woven in colour'; this conjecture would restore a form lost through confusion of abbreviations or minim strokes.

68–9. A coloured initial adorns line 69, *Now the kyng of this kythe kepe hym oure lorde*, though these probably represent scribal rather than authorial divisions. If the exordium of line 69 is not embroidered on the king's pavilion with the anglicized motto of the Order of the Garter (*honi soit qui mal y pense*), it is left floating unsatisfactorily as Gollancz's 'loyal exclamation on the part of the poet'.

71. The *wodwyse* is a mysterious figure who plays no active role in the poem other than to bear the royal arms of England on his lambrequin, the mantling that hangs from the back of his helmet. The wild man was a popular figure of untamed strength in medieval pageantry, art, heraldry, and literature, persisting in folk-ritual in parts of Europe until the eighteenth and nineteenth centuries (R. Bernheimer, *Wild Men in the Middle Ages* (Cambridge, Mass., 1952)). Closer to our period, Froissart tells in his *Chroniques* the much-quoted story of Charles VI's nearly fatal *Bal des Ardents* of 1393, when the king and several of his lords were dressed in costumes of wax and fur which caught fire. Similar scenes of royal pageantry must have been enacted in England, as the king's Wardrobe Accounts for 1345 note the production of various costumes for the king's Christmas plays at Oxford, including visors with *xij capita de wodewose* (N. H. Nicolas, 'Observations on the Institution of the Most Noble Order of the Garter', *Archeologia*, xxxi (1846), p. 43). Wild men were also popular as heraldic devices or ornaments embroidered on costumes, as the same accounts show. The *wodwyse* here appears in the traditional costume of curly tufts of fur or hair (*wrethyn lokkes*) but also wearing helmet and heraldic mantling, juxtaposing the symbols of his wild existence in the forest with his role in courtly ritual and pageantry.

78. **before and behynde:** These adverbs denote the first and last (that is, the top left and bottom right) quarters of the heraldic shield. The usage is rare, though not unknown in French and English, and the poet extends the analogy in line 80, where *one lofte* and *on lowe vndir* refer less elegantly to the second and third quarters. Edward III quartered the royal arms of France, the fleurs-de-lis or *flowres of Fraunse*, with those of England in 1337 when he took up his claim to the French throne. Richard II wore the same arms until 1394, when he impaled them with the arms of his patron saint, Edward the Confessor.

79. **with orfraied bestes:** *Orfraied* is an editorial conjecture to replace the manuscript reading *with sex grym bestes* which gives the aa/xx pattern in a line alliterating only on *Ynglonde* and the preposition *out*, with no compensating couplet alliteration. The conjectural *orfraied* derives from the OF noun *orfrois* which is glossed by *MED* 'Embroidered or bordered with gold; richly embroidered or bordered'. The word forms part of a distinct heraldic vocabulary: the first recorded use of the adjective comes as late as 1415, although the noun *orfroi* is used in England from the first half of the twelfth century.

*Orfraied* may well have been replaced by a scribe mistaking it for a form of 'afraid' and confident of correcting this apparent slight on the English lions. *Sex grym* bears all the hallmarks of a deliberate scribal substitution for a misunderstood or rejected word or phrase: it is emphatic, unmetrical and, given the following line, redundant.

83. **knyghte:** The manuscript's *kynge* is rejected for Gollancz's correction to *knyghte*, since the herald addressed by the king at line 101 is clearly standing next to the pavilion, while the king himself, whom the narrator does not see until line 86, is seated inside. Thornton makes a similar error in *The Parlement of the Thre Ages* 529, where *knyghtes* is confirmed by the Ware manuscript. Line 83 could thus be translated 'And I recognized the knight I saw next to the pavilion.'

90ff. Gollancz wishes to identify the king's clothes with robes worn by Edward III at the Feast of St George in 1351, robes which were similarly decorated with bird and garter embroidery. Nevertheless, the Wardrobe Accounts for other years (1347–8, 1360, 1363–4, 1374 etc.) also record the production of other robes worked with the Garter motto, hundreds of garters and other elaborate robes for the court. The clothes of this king actually represent a mixture of styles. Cloaked in loose, flowing kirtle and mantle, he does not follow the mid-century trend of tight-fitting garments, yet displays the fashionable opulence of exotic embroidery. Newton finds no mention of kirtles in the Wardrobe Accounts for this period and suggests that the word had become sufficiently archaic to be used romantically by fourteenth-century poets (p. 33). Newton goes on to remark that in this period 'the growing taste for embroidered decoration sometimes makes it difficult to distinguish what was theatrical, fanciful and exotic fashionable dress from what was made to wear at a joust'.

91. The description of the king's clothing is one of the most corrupt passages in the poem, and line 91, *Bery-brown was his berde brouderde with fewlys*, is most obviously at fault. Gollancz reads *Bery-brown [as] his berde*, but the comparison between the colour of the king's clothes and beard seems strained. Lines 91–7 contain a number of minor scribal corrections and larger, uncorrected errors while there is considerable inducement to *-de* in the middle of each line (*brouderde*, *golde*, *flakerande*, etc.): *berde* most likely anticipates *brouderde*. Turville-Petre's solution, glossing the manuscript line 'his clothes embroidered with birds', evades the problem. The present reconstruction, *Bery broun was [the bleaunt]*, is modelled on *Sir Gawain and the Green Knight* 879, *a meré mantyle . . . Of a broun bleeaunt enbrauded ful ryche.*

94. **gerede full riche:** Schumacher's phrase, used earlier in the poem at line 63, replaces the manuscript's *girde in the myddes*, which the scribe anticipated from the following line. Turville-Petre's retention of the manuscript reading, describing the garters 'wrapped around the middle of the birds', seems improbable.

97. **daderande þam semede:** *þam* is a dative form used with nominative function with an impersonal verb, as at line 176 below, while *seem* is a verb in a state of transition from an impersonal to a personal function (see T. F. Mustanoja, *A Middle English Syntax* (Helsinki, 1960), vol. I, pp. 112–13). Jerry D. James finds an implicit criticism of the king in the depiction on his belt of waterbirds pursued by falcons, 'these common birds cowering in fear of the royal falcon', as if the king surrounds himself with base creatures ('The Undercutting of Conventions in *Wynnere and Wastoure*', *MLQ*, xxv (1964), p. 250). On the other hand, this detail evokes the skill of the robe's designers, such that the birds appear to be trembling, and might exemplify the detailed 'pointing' which Burrow isolates as a characteristic feature of late fourteenth-century style (*Ricardian Poetry* (London, 1971), pp. 69ff.).

The king shares his love of hawking and hunting (lines 99–100) with Ȝouthe in *The Parlement of the Thre Ages*, and there are a number of parallels between the attractive pictures of Ȝouthe, the king, and the herald and, in certain aspects, Wastoure himself. (Conversely, Wynnere shares many preoccupations with Medill Elde.) The negative side of the figure of the Pride of Life is of course his prodigality. See Mary Dove, *The Perfect Age of Man's Life* (Cambridge, 1986).

103. **Thynke I dubbede the knyghte with dynttis to dele:** the double alliteration in the b-verse compensates for the single alliterating stress on *knyghte* in the a-verse of this unique instance of ax/aa alliteration.

108. **Ȝis lorde:** Gollancz argues that the scribe's exemplar read *Yserue*, in a northern form *ser*, which was then abbreviated to *Ys(er)*, which in turn would suggest *Yis*. The manuscript line is perfectly defensible, however, and there is no reason to assume a copyist's error. We may compare *Patience* 347, 'Ȝisse, lorde,' quoþ þe lede, 'lene me þy grace . . .' (ed. J. J. Anderson (Manchester, 1969)). Salter also draws attention to the formulaic quality of the second half-line *while my life dures* as a possible heraldic motto, or devise (pp. 53, 64, n. 92).

Gollancz, however, was keen to identify the herald as the Black Prince, and argues that *Yserue* would be an 'Englishing' of the Prince's motto, *Ich dene*. He had been researching the origin and correct form of this motto when he came to prepare his edition, and it would seem he was over-anxious to confirm the historical background of the poem and find there an anglicized version of the motto. (See S. Trigg, 'Israel Gollancz's *Wynnere and Wastoure*: Political Satire or Editorial Politics?' in *Medieval English Religious and Ethical Literature: Essays in Honour of G. H. Russell*, ed. Gregory Kratzmann and James Simpson (Cambridge, 1986), pp. 115–27.)

109ff. The herald is praised in a manner befitting a hero of romance as he arms himself for battle. D. S. Brewer points out that the traditional method of describing a warrior arming himself runs counter to the normal pattern of the rhetorical *descriptio*, which moves from head to foot ('The Arming of the Warrior in European Literature and Chaucer', in *Chaucerian Problems and*

*Perspectives: Essays Presented to Paul E. Beichner*, ed. E. Vasta and Z. P. Thundy (Notre Dame, 1979), pp. 221–43).

116. **chechun:** a unique form in Middle English, representing a regular aphetic development from the Anglo-Norman *eschucoun* (*AND escuchoun* s.).

117. **Thre wynges inwith wroghte in the kynde:** Gollancz contends that the herald's *thre wynges . . . wroghte in the kynde* are not wings, rather the ostrich feathers of the Black Prince's 'badge for peace'. Citing OE *feþera* pl. 'wings' he suggests that the terms 'wings' and 'feathers' may have coalesced in Middle English, and argues that the Prince's feather badge would be especially appropriate on this mission of peace. Salter comments firstly that there is no record of the Prince wearing this device on a jupon, and secondly, that the Prince's badge is always blazoned in English as bearing the 'plume' or 'feather', a literal translation of Latin *penna* or French *plume*. Furthermore, the phrase *in the kynde* makes poor sense in reference to feathers whereas heraldic wings may be borne in a variety of ways, some highly stylized, but some more natural (cf. *MED kinde* n., 4(c) and Salter, pp. 50–1, 53–4).

Salter none the less maintains that the herald's jupon is a 'distinguishing feature of some precision' and proposes that a member of the Wingfield family served as a model for the herald. Yet the poet's heraldic references remain suggestive rather than literal: we are not told the tincture of the field of the knight's jupon, nor is mention made of any ordinaries on the field. A reference to the *bend gules* on the Wingfield coat of arms would give greater support to Salter's theory. As it is, wings are a common heraldic charge, like the boars' heads on the banner of the Carmelites and cannot in themselves direct us to any individual.

118. **vmbygon with a gold wyre:** gold thread was used to appliqué the charges onto the jupon: its seams might also have been stitched over with this thread (Salter, pp. 63–4, n. 89).

119. **What! he was ʒongeste of ʒeris and ʒapeste of witt:** *What* is used here as an exclamation, as in the Knight's cry: '*What, welcome be the cut, a Goddes name!*' (*Gen. Prol.* 854, cited by *OED What* B.I.1). Gollancz translates 'When the warrior I knew, Lo, he was youngest of years. . . .' But for *What* to have its full exclamatory power, we must read *knewe* as 'recognized', translating 'When I recognized that man—well! he was the youngest in years and keenest of wit that anyone in the world knew of his age (*or*, of his generation).'

*ʒape* is used several times of *ʒouthe* in *The Parlement of the Thre Ages*, and also in *Sir Gawain and the Green Knight* to describe the youthful court, the New Year, and Arthur himself.

121. **brayde:** The manuscript's *caughten* fulfils the demands of neither alliteration (giving the pattern aa/xx) nor inflectional agreement: its sense is weak and *caughten* is almost certainly the unconscious substitution of an inattentive scribe. Gollancz proposes reading *caughte* or *brawndeschet*, while Schumacher suggests *broughte*. *Brayde*, from OE *bregdan*, can mean 'seize,

grasp, reach for, tear or break something by pulling', and *MED* gives an apt example under *breiden* v.(1), 8, from *The Life of St. Anne*; *An anngell ... a braunche of gon brayd.* Another sense not given by *MED*, 'unfurl a banner', is attested by three examples in *Wynnere and Wastoure* (lines 52, 149, 163), and *brayde* seems a feasible reading here. It is exactly the kind of regular b-verse of weak sense that the scribe was most likely to replace: see line 94 above, and his own corrections at lines 16, 50, 184, and 195.

125. **Sendes erande by me als hym beste lyketh:** Gollancz's emendation of *Send his* to *sendes* is adopted here, as the manuscript's *Send* would be an unlikely contracted form. Perhaps Thornton omitted an abbreviation symbol for *-es.*

Even though the single alliterating syllable in the a-verse falls on a preposition, the line forms part of a couplet on *b* with the following line, and Gollancz's emendation of *erande* to *bodworde* is unnecessary. Kölbing would reconstruct the entire line to read *Send his sonde by me als hym semes beste.*

126ff. The herald's speech has been interpreted as a precise allusion to the Statute of Treasons promulgated in 1352 which condemns the practice of leading personal bands of armed men. Salter shows that if this is indeed the case, the poet has radically misunderstood the crucial terms of the statute (pp. 41–3). Drafted under William Shareshull as Chief Justice, it carefully distinguishes between the crimes of high and petty treason. Thereafter the act of leading a band of armed men against another band, but not against the king, was to be interpreted as felony or trespass, not treason. The punishment for either offence was death and forfeiture of property; this went to the culprit's lord if the offence was judged felonous or to the king if judged treasonable.

The situation in *Wynnere and Wastoure* is imprecise in comparison, as the herald threatens the leaders with loss of land and life for abrogating the king's privilege of riding with banners displayed and disturbing his peace, without revealing who will receive their forfeited property. It is only later that they are recognized as members of the king's household; at this stage they are spoken of as foreigners who are promised pardon because they are ignorant of the law. Salter concludes that 'from a strictly legalistic point of view, the only reign during which the activities of Wynnere and Wastoure could unequivocally have been interpreted as treason, and punishable to the harshest degree of the law ... was that of Richard II, and even then, after 1381' (p. 43). In that year, Richard extended the definition of treason by Parliamentary Statute to include the offence of which Wynnere and Wastoure appear to be charged. We are doubtless treading on uncertain ground, and have no way of knowing whether the reference is vague because the poet misunderstood the terms of the Statute, or intended only a general allusion or was indeed writing much later. The situation is further complicated by the crown's actual understanding of the treason laws which at times made a mockery of such nice distinctions propounded by the Statute. During the fourteenth and fifteenth centuries, the English kings 'continued to hold that it only needed an act of arms and a banner displayed to make riot an act of treason' (J. G. Bellamy, *The Law of Treason in England in the Later Middle Ages* (Cambridge, 1970), p. 48). Given this unstable element, line 130, *For this es the vsage here and euer schall worthe*, probably indicates the poet's understanding of the laws not as they were formulated but as they were seen to operate, and the emphasis in the preceding lines probably falls on the crime itself rather than its legal definition.

The phrase *his pese to disturbe* might be a deliberate echo of Shareshull's speech to the Parliament in 1352, declaring the causes of summoning the Parliament. These included the prevalence of armed bands of riotours:

... Pur ceo que nostre Seignour le Roi ad entenduz que la pees de son Roialme n'est pas bien garde come estre deveroit, et que les destourbours de la Pees et meintenours des quereles et des riotes faites en pais grevont trop a son poeple, sanz ceo que due punissement est fait de eux.

*(Rotuli Parliamentorum*, II. 236–7)

Although the phrase 'to disturb the peace' is recorded in other documents of this period, its repetition at line 317 as part of Wastoure's abuse of Shareshull alerts us to the likelihood that the poet makes some kind of reference to the Statute here (see also Commentary on line 317 below).

127. **ne stirre:** While the manuscript's *no* can mean 'nor' as the sense requires (*MED no* conj.), the normal usage of this poem requires *ne* (cf. Glossary). The scribe either misread his exemplar, mistaking *e* for *o*, or anticipated his copy, catching *no* from *none*.

129. **with ȝoure powers:** The shift from third to second person is not a scribal irregularity here but a deliberate change of register in the herald's tone from a statement of a general principle in lines 126–8 to its application in the present context in line 129. He then tactfully moves back into the third person when speaking of punishment, and reverts to the second in lines 134–5 to reassure the companies of the king's forgiveness of their trespass.

134. **kynge ryche:** 'the powerful king'. *Ryche* is an unusual spelling, and the *y* has presumably been caught from *kythe* and *kynge*. The alternative, of reading *kynge ryche* as a compound 'kingdom', leaves the pronoun *he* in line 135 without an antecedent noun.

136. **thies wyes amonges:** The manuscript reading, *Full wyde hafe I walked amonges thies wyes one* is corrected here to ... *thies wyes amonges*, '(I have travelled widely) among these people'. We are alerted to the possibility of scribal error in the repetition of *one* from the preceding line, while there is no great gain in sense in having the herald walking 'alone': the syntax is also uncharacteristically diffuse. The present reconstruction preserves the alliterative pattern of the original reading: and again, we note Thornton's apparent carelessness with the second, weaker half of the line.

138–42. It is not absolutely clear from the text that the contingents from Europe are all part of Wynnere's army. They have come from countries well known as England's trading partners, and the *Estirlynges*, or Hanseatic merchants, certainly invite such an association, but Wynnere's task will be to raise money for the king's wars in France, and it is difficult to see why the French should be ranged on his side. This account of the armies is perhaps a more general allusion to the extraordinary and international nature of the problems to be raised in the debate. Line 143, '*And ʒondere a banere . . .*', thus opens the formal identification of the two armies.

143–8. The appearance of the pope both here and in the king's summing-up is a further example of the general resentment of papal wealth and power witnessed throughout the fourteenth century. In Wynnere's army, the pope is certainly a symbolic rather than an individualized figure, and Gollancz's attempt to identify him as Clement VI seems misguided. Historical precedent for such pageantry is found in a tournament held at Smithfield in 1343, when the king as a knight bachelor formed with his companions a group dressed as the pope and twelve cardinals; on other occasions they dressed as Tartars, and once formed a group comprising a mayor and his aldermen (Newton, p. 41).

144. **bulles:** The manuscript's *bibulles* is rejected here in favour of Gollancz's emendation to *bulles*. Although bibles would be an appropriate papal charge, the orthography of *bible* admits little variety in Middle English (*MED bible* n.), and the manuscript's emphasis on the second syllable indicates textual confusion: *bibulles* may represent scribal repetition or deliberate re-writing. Furthermore, the cords and seals are more appropriate to papal documents than bibles.

149–55. The banner of the lawyers and judges bears the charge of three carefully groomed and coiffed heads. Lawyers' coifs figure in Wastoure's abuse of the legal profession at line 314, while the *bende of grene* may be an allusion to the seal on a writ, the 'green wax' which often features in satirical poems. If a writ was not sealed, the sheriff was under oath not to accept it, yet the cost was a penny for writing and sixpence for sealing and the green wax as a source of revenue for lawyers thus became a symbol of hatred and mistrust of the legal profession (*Mum and the Sothsegger*, ed. M. Day and R. Steele, EETS, 199 (1936), p. xxvii).

156–87. The friars' banners were the subject of heated debate early this century between H. Bradley and G. Neilson. The latter was attempting to link the banners to the arms of the friars' patrons or friends and associates of the poem's supposed author, Huchown. This research has been completely discredited, but the exchange makes curious reading: see particularly G. Neilson, *The Athenaeum*, 26. Oct. 1901, 16 May, 13 June, 15 Aug. 1903; H. Bradley, 23 May, 27 June.

These and other scholars have interpreted the charges on the banners as a focus for anti-mendicant satire, though most of the charges are conventional, and such readings often seem strained (see Gollancz's Commentary). For instance, the boars' heads on the Carmelites' banner have been read as signifying their gluttony, yet this banner is praised as *þe faireste of þam alle* and is moreover specifically associated with the Virgin.

157. **galegs:** Gollancz interprets manuscript *galeys* as a deliberate substitution for *galegs* 'sandals', although Stern rightly considers it more probable that *g* was mistaken for *y* in the scribe's exemplar. The *brases* and *bokels* of line 158 suggest footwear rather than ships or gallows and *MED* (*galoche* n.) cites many variant spellings of this word. A *galeg*, or *galoche*, is a simple sandal, and seems to have been acceptable among the friars as a substitute for going barefoot.

163. **was:** As at lines 167, 176, 187, and 188 below, Gollancz emends the tense so that the herald speaks entirely in the present. In line 163, there may have been inducement to *was* from *wanne* in the preceding line, but this edition accepts such variety in narrative tense as authorial.

164. **balle:** Bradley's suggestion that manuscript *balke* should read *balle* has been adopted by all editors (*The Athenaeum*, 121 (23 May 1903), pp. 657–8.

166. **mayne:** The manuscript line is unsatisfactory by any standard: *When it hase most of þe maye on missomer euen.* *Maye* seems to have lost a mark of nasal suspension to give *mayne*, which takes the sense 'virtue, efficacy' when applied to astronomical bodies such as the sun. Further, when the sun is employed as an heraldic charge, it is depicted as 'a globe of gold with the lineaments of a human face, surrounded by rays, alternately waved and straight' (J. Woodward, *A Treatise on Heraldry*, Edinburgh, 1892, rpt. 1969, p. 306), and is blazoned as 'in his splendour, in his glory', phrases which are echoed by the reconstructed line, *When it hase moste of þe mayne.*

In a recent note Nicholas Havely revives Bradley's hypothesis that the Dominicans' banner features elements from Dominican hagiography and iconography, but concludes by finding greater significance in the irony of the Dominicans' 'tacit admission that their energies are enlisted in the cause of *wynnynge*' ('The Dominicans and Their Banner in *Wynnere and Wastoure*', *N&Q*, n.s. xxx (1983), pp. 207–9: see also Havely, 'Chaucer's Friar and Merchant', *Chaucer Review*, xiii (1979), pp. 337–45).

176, 186. Although the arms and banners are only loosely symbolic, there are sufficient internal references to suggest that lines 176 and 186 have been transposed by a scribe. The Carmelites or White Friars were known for their devotion to the Virgin, the protector of their order, so that the manuscript's line 186, *Be any crafte þat I kan Carmes thaym semyde*, would most naturally precede the line which describes the friars as those who love to serve *oure lady* (line 177). The banner described in line 175 as *blee whitte with three bore hedes* could apply in such a vague heraldic context either to the Carmelites or the Augustinians. The sixth banner described in lines 180–7 is also white, but charged with black belts buckled together, and this would be particularly appropriate to the Augustinian friars whose habit was black with a leather girdle. The herald indeed remarks on the belts as he identifies the banner.

The substitution would seem to be accidental, while the similarity in colour of the two banners and the repetitive, formal method of blazoning the banners may have occasioned the error.

177. **ledis:** The manuscript's *ordire* disrupts the alliterative pattern in this line, as the poet seems to allow the variant xa/ax only when voiced/unvoiced or couplet alliteration is involved. The possibility of vocalic alliteration can be discounted as only one stressed syllable would thus bear alliteration. The line also demands a plural subject for *louen*. *Ordire* may have been caught from line 186 after a previous scribe had transposed lines 176 and 186 or may indeed represent a deliberate substitution of a specific, technically accurate word for the more general term. *Ledes* was first proposed by Kölbing, but *ledis* is the usual spelling of the word in this text (lines 88, 152, 171, etc.).

179. **shall:** In the manuscript, the *ha* of *shall* appears to be written over *al*. Thornton was clearly on the point of writing the northern form *sall*, as at line 369. The textual uncertainty which surrounds lines 176–86 is underlined by the several false starts in the manuscript at lines 179, 181, and 184.

183–5. The points which are *pared off rownde* are the ends of the belts which hang down after passing through the buckles, tapered off to a neat round end. *Pendant* was another word for the hanging end of a belt, which seems to have been tucked away neatly out of sight (*awaye*). Most editors emend to *pendant*[*s*], to form a parallel with the other plural nouns, but *pendant* may simply represent a narrative shift from the specific to the general. Cf. the Laud *Troy Book*: *Eche man . . . takes gerdeles of riche barres / With bokeles of gold and fair pendaunt*, lines 8241–3.

186. See note to line 176 above.

187, 188. **knewe, seghe:** See note to line 163 above.

189–90. *Some wittnesse of wolle:* Stern alone retains the manuscript reading of line 189, *Some of wittnesse of wolle . . .*, taking *wittnesse* as a noun parallel to *synes* in line 188. I have assumed that the scribe caught the first *of* from the following line, and reconstructed the text thus:

> Some witnesse of wolle and some of wyne tounnes
> Some of merchandes merke[s] so many and so thikke. . . .

Gollancz offers a more complicated reconstruction, [*And oþer*] *of merchandes merke*[*s*], arguing that wool and winecasks are merchant signs, and the manuscript's distinction between them is unnecessary. Even so, the herald makes it clear that while he can discern a few recognizable emblems for wool and wineguilds, the remainder are so numerous that he is bewildered. Turville-Petre reads manuscript *merke* in line 190 as a verb, but *MED* offers no confirmation of this sense. If we keep *merke* as a noun and correct to the plural the syntax is somewhat clumsy but does not warrant correction on the scale proposed by Gollancz.

A helpful account of medieval economics is J. L. Bolton, *The Medieval English Economy, 1150–1500* (London, 1980). Certainly the wool industry was crucial to England's prosperity in this period.

193–6. The disproportionate account of Wastoure's army has left many readers wondering if the poet has not simply run out of inspiration, and Bestul reminds us that Wynnere's army includes the traditional figures of venality satire. N. Jacobs, on the other hand, interprets this imbalance as a sign of the poet's general bias in favour of Wastoure, 'The Typology of Debate and the Interpretation of *Wynnere and Wastoure*', *RES*, n. s. xxxvi (1985), 481–500.

Wastoure's army is described, to be sure, in terms of approbation and admiration (*And sekere one þat other syde are sadde men of armes*), yet it has also been associated with the armed bands of riotours and robbers whose activity the 1352 Treasons Statute was designed to inhibit and who are mentioned in Shareshull's speech to the Parliament in 1352 as *Les destourbours de la Pees et meintenours des quereles et des riotes.* We might also compare the earlier Statute of 1331: *Diverses roberies, homicides, & felonies, ont este faitz einz ces heures par gentz qi sont appelleȝ Roberdesmen, Wastours & Draghlacche* (Act 5, Edward III, cited by *OED* under *Roberdsmen* s.v.). Wasters in *Piers Plowman* are similarly associated with vagrancy, and it is true that the leaders of criminal gangs were often members of the gentry, that is, knights and squires, operating through networks of bastard feudality (J. G. Bellamy, *Crime and Public Order in England in the Later Middle Ages*, London, 1973, p. 72). Wastoure's railing against Shareshull at line 317 might confirm this association, but conversely, Wynnere can be accused of precisely the same offence—leading a personal army.

197. **that thaym hedir broghte:** the aa/xa pattern here seems to be introduced as deliberate variation. *Hedir* also echoes the previous line's alliteration on *h*.

201. **wye:** Manuscript *wyes* must be an error for the singular form: the final *-e* may have been mistaken for *-s*, and thus taken as a plural inflection.

**demeth:** The manuscript's *doeth* makes no sense, and probably results from scribal confusion of *e* and *o*, and the omission of a macron indicating suspension of *m* in the exemplar. As an unfamiliar form of *Tharf*, 'need', *Thare* may have caused further confusion.

205–6. These lines were used by Gollancz to confirm a composition date of 1352–3, for Edward III came to the throne in 1328. But even if we were to accept the historical identity of the king, the phrase *fyve and twenty wyntere* appears as an alliterating phrase in a form which the scribal tradition cannot be trusted to have reproduced accurately. The half-line is unusual in having three unstressed syllables between the stressed syllables; ironically, Gollancz shows himself inconsistent in his metrical policies by not rejecting this line as hypermetrical, especially as numerical formulas are frequently miscopied in textual transmission, more so if roman numerals are used at any stage.

Allowing for its originality, though, similar round numbers in medieval poetry often signify nothing more precise than 'a long time' or 'a lifetime'. One example from *Piers Plowman* will suffice: in most A-text manuscripts, Piers says he has followed Truth for *fourty wynter*, while other manuscripts read *foure*, *fiftene* or *seuenty* (A. VI. 30).

211. **henttis by þe handes:** *henttis* and *hetys* take *þam* in the second clause as their direct object, an example of what Mustanoja calls the 'non-expression of the object-pronoun' (Mustanoja, p. 144).

212. **welcomes:** a rare example of the intransitive function of the verb, as in *OED Welcome v.*[2] 'to be welcome'. *OED* cites only Lovelich's *Grail* xlii, 278–80, *Ful lowde to hem they gonne to Crye, and seide 'welcometh' Al An hye . . . 'Welcometh' quod Iosephes ful Sekerly. Welcomes* is a comparable example of the imperative plural with a Northern inflection, and we need not emend with Gollancz to produce the interjection *Welcome.*

**hyne of oure house bothen:** For a stimulating analysis of *Wynnere and Wastoure* in terms of the economical structure of the royal household, see David Starkey, 'The Age of the Household: Politics, Society and the Arts, c.1350–c.1550', in *The Later Middle Ages*, ed. S. Medcalf (London, 1981), pp. 225–90.

213. **askes:** Again we note the mixture of present and past tenses.

215. **sowrede:** Gollancz rejected *sowrede* as an error for *sowede*, a rare word of uncertain origin (*OED Sow v.*[2] 'pain, grieve'), yet *sowrede* derives from OE *sūr*, adj. (*OED Sow v.*). Clark Hall and Meritt also give *(a)sūrian* and *sūrēagede.*

217. **Full:** from ME *ful*, adj. or alternatively, a Western dialectal form of *fillen*, as in *Piers Plowman* A. XI. 44, *And gnawen god in [þe gorge] whenne here guttis fullen.*

The call for drinks is repeated at lines 366–7 and has been regarded as an ironic comment on the action of the poem, following the king's offer of wine and then the account of Wastoure's feast. The repeated lines seem to be a stylistic remnant of the minstrel's art; certainly the fitt divisions perform little formal or structural function as the poem is too short (barely longer than a single fitt of *Sir Gawain and the Green Knight*) and its action too continuous to require these pauses. The lines calling for wine are part of the poet's overall fiction, reminding us of the dreamer's presence, like the address to the readers at line 31.

225. **littill-whattes:** the more common phrase in Middle English is *litel what* or *littles what.* The poet seems to have coined a new plural expression.

227. **gadir:** Burrow was the first to recognize the poet's intransitive use of *gadir* 'accumulate'; see *MED gaderen* v.1(a) 'assemble' and *OED Gather v.* II, *intr.* 19.

230. **witt:** *Witt* gradually shifts in sense throughout this speech from 'skill, knowledge' to 'craft, guile' to Wynnere's climax at line 230, *Alle þat I wynn thurgh witt he wastes thurgh pryde.* The poet often exploits the binary structure

of his line in this way to define a contrast between the two opponents in lines which rapidly acquire a proverbial or mnemonic cadence. The very opposition between *pryde* and *witt* confirms the latter's negative aspect and hints at its frequently ironic overtones. We may compare *Piers Plowman* A. V. 114–27 and Coveitise's confession of the 'lessons' he learnt in his apprenticeship in the merchant trade.

231–2. Further rhetorical and rhythmical oppositions between Wynnere and Wastoure are developed in these lines; we may compare Matthew of Vendôme's example of 'antithesis', a prodigal confronting a miser:

> Prandeo, jejunas; do, quaeris; gaudeo, maeres;
> Poto, sitis; retines, erogo; spero, times.
>
> (*Ars Versificatoria*, 3.25, ed. E. Faral, *Les Arts Poétiques du XII<sup>e</sup> et du XIII<sup>e</sup> siècle: recherches et documents sur la technique littéraire du moyen âge*, Paris, 1924)

Bestul also compares Dante, *Inf.* 7.28–33 and the exchange of verbal abuse between the avaricious and the prodigal (p. 16).

**I pryke and I pryne:** Burrow compares the phrase 'pick and preen', used of birds trimming their feathers, and translates 'I make everything trim and tidy(?)', an interpretation echoed in Turville-Petre's gloss, 'I assemble it neatly'. But Gollancz is closer to the mark when he translates 'I pin and sew up'. *Pryke* and *pryne* are virtually synonymous, meaning 'fasten, secure, sew, pin'. *Pryke* (late OE *prician*) is used of fastening something with a pin or skewer (*MED pricken* v.), while *pryne*, from OE *prēon* 'pin, brooch', is now a Scots and northern dialect word which means 'sew, stitch up' (*MED prenen* v.). Wynnere's metaphor describes his attempts to secure the wealth which Wastoure expends: *I pryke and I pryne and he the purse opynes.*

236. **The deuyll wounder the wele:** The manuscript reads *The deuyll wounder one the wele*, perhaps a scribal attempt to make *wounder* into a verb by adding the preposition *one*. *The deuyll wounder* is a phrase analogous with expressions such as 'small wonder', 'great wonder', found in Old and Middle English (*OED Wonder sb.* 6d, e). This reconstruction assumes with Gollancz and Burrow that the scribe's correction is a pedantic improvement.

237. **hungere:** Hungere is virtually personified at line 237 and recalls Langland's fuller development of Hungere and his inevitable association with Wasters in *Piers Plowman*, A. VII.

**heghe howses:** Gollancz blames scribal inducement to *how-* from *howndes* and *dowfehowses* in line 235 for the loss of an original *horses*, arguing from the frequency of the phrase *heghe horse* in alliterative poetry. But as Rosenfield comments, we need assume merely that Wastoure's high buildings are unlet for Wynnere's criticism of his household management to be perfectly consistent. Burrow describes the houses as a sign of extravagant impracticality, comparing similar lines in *Mum and the Sothsegger* (3. 216–18). The manuscript reading finds further support from line 289 when Wynnere exhorts Wastoure, *Rayse vp thi renthowses*, and line 438 when Wastoure in turn condemns Wynnere's lack of expenditure on his property, *ʒe nade hightilde vp ʒour houses*.

248. One of Wastoure's favourite strategies is to identify Wynnere as the avaricious merchant familiar from homiletic *exempla* who cannot sleep for worrying about his wealth, and the prospect of its dispersal after his death (compare lines 298–301, 443–4 below). We may compare ʒouthe's description of Medill Elde's preoccupations in *The Parlement of the Thre Ages*, lines 257–60 (*And thou with wandrynge and woo schalte wake for thi gudes*), and Jean de Meun's earlier satire on the merchant laden with anxiety in the speech of Raison, *Le Roman de la Rose* (lines 4975–5182).

249. **And iche a wy in this werlde that wonnes the abowte:** this should be read as if in parentheses, an afterthought to the subject *thou* in line 248.

254. **Some rote, some ruste:** cf. Matt. vi. 19–21.

256. Wastoure reminds Wynnere of the duty the rich owe the poor, and we are again reminded of *Piers Plowman*, and Patience's promise of Christ's mercy *if ye riche haue ruþe and rewarde wel þe poore* (B. XIV. 145).

264. **thou:** Manuscript *tho* is recorded by *OED* as a form of *Though* (adv. and conj.), which would give the reading 'You speak of a grievance although (you) caused it yourself', with omission of the subject-pronoun. However, the conjunction in *Wynnere and Wastoure* is elsewhere spelled *þofe* (cf. line 420), and Kölbing's restoration of the pronoun *thou* completes the line so that the second half neatly answers the first: 'You speak of a grievance; you caused it yourself'.

266. **wayttinge:** manuscript *playinge* seems to be a deliberate scribal substitution for an unfamiliar or illegible reading. The line not only lacks alliteration in an important position without the support of complementary alliteration in an adjacent line, but also its weak sense indicates scribal interference. The proposed reconstruction *wayttinge* 'feasting, entertainment' employs a rare word which, according to *OED* (s.v. *Waiting vbl.sb.*[2]), is found only in *Cursor Mundi* and then only in some manuscripts at lines 3343–4 (*Ilk mane gaue he sumkin thing, / And batuel made fair waiting*) and 12543–5 (*Ai quen iosep was wont at weind / Til any waiting wit sum frend, / His suns war ai wit him bun*). Both examples are from the Cotton manuscript, although the Göttingen text also reads *waiting* at line 12544. The other manuscripts read *gest(e)nyng*. *OED* compares modern Icel. *veitingar* pl. 'entertainment' and *veita* 'give a feast' from Old Norse *veita* 'give, grant' (cf. also ON *veita veizlu* 'give a feast', and *OED Wait v.*[2]). A scribe to whom this word was unfamiliar would probably interpret it as a form of *wayte* 'keep vigil, watching' from ONF *waitier*, and an error which needed correction; *playinge* would seem to fit the context.

*Wayttinge* 'feasting' is more appropriate to the context than any of the solutions proposed by other editors and commentators who concede corruption in the line: *wraxling(e)* (Kölbing, Gollancz, Kaiser, Haskell); *wrastlinge* (Berry);

*waltering* (Schumacher) or *wastinge* (Holthausen). Stern, Burrow, and Turville-Petre read *playinge* but the line offers a dramatic example of the poor text which can result from refusing to emend on alliterative grounds.

267. **angarte pryde:** To avoid a two-syllable 'dip' in the b-verse, Gollancz emends to *angarte of pryde*, reading *angarte* as a noun. However, the word is used elsewhere as an adjective (*MED angard* n. (b)), and the manuscript reading does not warrant correction.

The etymology of *angarte* is much debated. *OED* (s.v. *angart*) suggests the word is a perversion of ON *ágjart*, neut. of *ágjarn* 'ambitious, insolent', while Cyril Brett derives the word from OF *angarde* 'vantage; eminence, height', presuming sense development analogous with *hauteur* and confusion with Middle English *ouergart*, from Modern Icel. *gort* 'pride' ('Notes on *Sir Gawayne and the Green Knight*', *MLR*, viii (1913), 160–4).

268. **wele:** The poet puns here on *wele* 'well, spring', and 'wealth'.

269. **grounden:** *Grounden* is a rare variant of *graunted* (s.v. *MED graunten* v.); there is no reason to emend to Holthausen's *graunted*. Burrow comments that the phrase 'given and granted' is a legalism rendering Latin *datum et concessum*.

270. **rychely:** this corrects manuscript *ryhely*.

275. **gleterand frostes:** Although he conceded the possibility of alliteration between voiced and unvoiced consonants, Schumacher proposed reading *cleterand* for *gleterand* in this line. Gollancz emends to *clengande* on the strength of *Sir Gawain and the Green Knight* 1694, *for þe forst clenged*.

Line 275 forms a couplet alliterating on *c* and *k* with the previous line, however, and the alliteration of voiced and unvoiced sounds in this context seems to be a stylistic feature of this poem.

The *dede monethe* in line 276 is March: lines 274–6 sum up the natural annual cycle of harvest before winter and the fallow period before the spring sowing. A. S. Daley ('Chaucer's "droghte of March" in Medieval Farm Lore', *Chaucer Review*, iv (1970), pp. 171–9) demonstrates that the *droghte of March* was a recognized feature of the English climate; the lack of rain was not unwelcome but made March the appropriate season for preparing and dressing the arable fields with manure and also for ploughing (wheat, rye, and oats were sown at this time). Piers names among his minimal equipment a cart *To drawe on feld my dong while þe drouȝt lastiþ* (A. VII. 272).

277. **thou wolle to the tauerne:** The verb 'to go' is understood here after *wolle*. Schumacher proposes the much heavier reading . . . *thou wolle [te] to the tauerne* on metrical grounds, and he is followed by Gollancz; but the alliteration on the preposition *to* is countered by full stresses on *tauerne* and *tonne*.

**tonne-hede:** All editors except Rosenfield transcribe these words as *toune-hede*, following Gollancz's argument that this is a northern dialect term for the upper extremity of a town. However, Gollancz cannot explain why a word localized by *EDD* in Northumberland, Lakeland, and North-West Derbyshire should indicate a part of London ('some locality near Shoreditch, or

Finsbury'). Moreover, it is difficult to find a satisfactory gloss for the preposition in the phrase *byfore þe toune-hede*.

Rosenfield's transcription *tonne-hede* 'tun-head' gives *byfore* a stronger sense. The manuscript also supports this reading, since 'town' is usually spelled *towne* or *townn* where 'tun' appears as *wyne tounnes* in line 189. *Tonne-hede* is not recorded elsewhere, but the compound is not a difficult one. *MED hed* n.(1), 7a gives 'The upper end, top . . . of a still, the still-head, condensing cap; of a barrel'.

277–82. Wynnere's scornful account of Wastoure at the tavern recalls the scene in *Piers Plowman* in which Gluttony stops off at the inn on his way to confession, even down to the reproduction of the shouts of the drinkers: *þere was lauȝing & louryng & 'lete go þe cuppe!'* (A. V. 185). We may also compare the later passage at VIII. 67–75 where the narrator associates wasters with itinerants and beggars in their promiscuity:

> þei wedde no womman þat hy wiþ delen
> But as wilde bestis wiþ wehe, & worþ vp togideris
>
> (lines 73–4)

It is possible that our poet borrows phrases from Langland's fuller scenes, particularly as Wynnere now exhorts Wastoure to tend to his lands and his ploughing, the very activity neglected by the wasters on Piers's half-acre.

279. **hete:** 'order, call for', a rare development from OE *hātan*, pa.t. *heht*, contracted to *het* (s.v. *OED Hight v.*). Cf. *Sir Gawain and the Green Knight* 2121, and line 211 above.

281. **florence:** Gollancz glosses *florence* as a woman's name, though this usage is not recorded before about 1700. *MED* lists *florence* as a plural form of OF *florin*, while D. C. Baker argues that florin was often used as a general word for money ('Gold Coins in Medieval English literature', *Speculum*, xxxvi (1961), 282–7). We may also compare *Piers Plowman* A. II. 108, *þanne fette fauel forþ floreynes ynowe.* This reading makes of line 281 a dialogue between Wastoure and the inn-keeper, 'Then there is no conversation except "fill up" and "pay up", to make you show your money.'

286. A loose reference to the story of Cain and Abel, Genesis iv. 4–5.

288. **tynen:** This reconstructed form replaces manuscript *tymen*, which is defended by Rosenfield and Stern as a reflex of OE *temian* 'tame' or 'subdue, compel' (s.v. *OED Teme v.*), even though neither sense is used of cultivating land.

Burrow also retains the manuscript reading but notes the verb *tine* 'harrow' (*OED Tine v.*[3]) and compares Modern English *tine* sb. 'prong of a harrow' which has a variant *time* in Modern Scots (*SND Tine* n.). This verb is recorded only from the eighteenth century, however, and while 'harrow' might seem to fit the context the manuscript form is best explained as an error, influenced by *rymen* in the following line, for *tynen*, 'fence, enclose'. This reading would represent the Old English verb *tỹnan* which has a continuous history in English (see *OED Tine, tyne v.*[1] and *EDD tine v.*[2]).

291–3. Wynnere predicts famine on earth and torment after death for Wastoure in 'the extreme cold which traditionally alternates with the extreme heat of the medieval hell' (Burrow).

295. **With oure festes and oure fare we feden the pore:** S. S. Hussey compares these lines with Mede's claim that lavish expenditure is necessary for the economic health of society ('Langland's Reading of Alliterative Poetry', *MLR* lx (1965), 167–8).

300. **Owthir freres it feche:** The manuscript reads *it freres it feche*, though this was initially read as *it freres feche* by Gollancz. Steadman notes the error in his review, while Gollancz's second edition adopted Kölbing's emendation to *Owthir it freres feche.* The first *it* was presumably caught from the second or from the preceding line.

302. **slees:** Gollancz misreads this as *sees* and emends to *sewes* in his first edition. Steadman noted the error but in the second edition, Gollancz still corrects *slees* to *sewes.* Manuscript *slees* can be successfully glossed 'destroys' (*OED Slay v.*[1]), as Wastoure argues that Wynnere's heirs and executors will ruin each other financially and spiritually in disputing the will.

304. **myndale:** Formed on analogy with 'church-ale', 'bride-ale', etc., the compound 'mind-ale' is unique here. *MED* compares OE *gemynd-dæg*, a day commemorating the anniversary of a person's death.

305. **A dale aftir thi daye:** It will not profit Wynnere's soul to leave large bequests to the poor in his will. This was a favourite doctrine of Archbishop Fitzralph of Armagh, and featured in the sermons he preached in London in 1356–7, sermons characterized by the vehemence of their attacks on the friars (K. Walsh, *Richard Fitzralph in Oxford, Avignon and Armagh* (Oxford, 1981), pp. 196, 200, 211, and 212).

311. **his fere one the ferrere syde:** Saturday, a fast-day in honour of the Virgin.

314. **bonets:** Most editors preserve the manuscript's *howes one lofte*, even though this gives the alliterative pattern aa/xx, a pattern rejected as scribal in this edition when it does not form part of an alliterative couplet. *Howes* appears to be a deliberate or unconscious substitution. Gollancz's conjectural reading is *biggins*, a sixteenth-century word for 'child's cap' which came to be used as hood or coif in the seventeenth century. An alternative conjecture is *bonets*, from the French word for a woollen fabric of which headgear was made (s.v. Godefroy, *bonet* s.m.). The word is used in Middle English to describe a cap or bonnet worn by men and women (s.v. *MED bonet* n., first recorded in the fifteenth century) and is also common in Middle Scots (cf. *DOST Bonet, Bonat* n.). Henryson seems to use it in a semi-technical sense for the *pileus* or pillion, a 'round and often close-fitting cap which was generally used to mark the possession of a doctoral degree' (*The Poems of Robert Henryson*, ed. D. Fox

(Oxford, 1981), notes to lines 1053 and 1353, pp. 247, 2660). In 'The Trial of the Fox', Henryson writes: '*This new-maid doctour off diuinite / With his reid cap can tell 30w weill aneuch*' (lines 1052–3). The wolf's cap is described a few lines later as *30ne reid bonat* (1061). Fox is of the opinion that Æsop's *bonat round . . . off the auld fassoun* (*Fables*, line 1353) may also be a *pileus*. If *bonet* was a late borrowing from Old French, it was probably unfamiliar to an early copyist of *Wynnere and Wastoure*, and replaced by the more familiar *howes* (cf. line 150 above). The initial letters of the two words can appear similar, and the scribe might have used *howes* to correct an apparent fault in his exemplar.

317. **Scharshull:** In her study of Sir William Shareshull, Bertha Putnam emphasizes his colourful career (he was dismissed as a judge and imprisoned in 1340 then later excommunicated for pronouncing a judgement against the Bishop of Ely), and his part in 'restrictive legislation of all kinds', including the Statute of Labourers of 1351 and the Treasons Statute of the following year (*The Place in Legal History of Sir William Shareshull* (Cambridge, 1950), p. 45). Putnam describes him as 'an object of hatred to the turbulent element in all classes of society' and mentions an incident in Hertfordshire in 1358 when a clerk and a group of men were indicted for various offences, including the clerk's words that they would all gladly strike Shareshull (p. 148). J. G. Bellamy records another, earlier incident in which a 'band of evil-doers' after sessions in Ipswich in 1344 proclaimed that Shareshull should appear before them under penalty of one hundred pounds (*Crime and Public Order*, p. 77).

The Chief Justice did in fact suffer several assaults on his person, servants, and property, and his assizes in Wiltshire were threatened by armed men in 1336. Nevertheless, it is worth noting that Putnam finds 107 variations in the spelling of his name and many cases of confusion with other judges, especially John Shardelow (d. 1344) and two with the names of Scardeburgh and Scorburgh. This confusion was 'catastrophic for his reputation as a judge' (p. 91).

If the lines in *Wynnere and Wastoure* were written after 1352, as seems likely despite Salter's reservations (see Commentary on line 126 above), they could have been inspired by Shareshull's reputation any time before his death in 1370, and possibly even later. He served as Chief Justice from 1350–61 and was still active in 1367. Born in 1289 or 1290 his longevity is remarkable, and may have contributed to his role as an object of attack.

Wastoure complains Shareshull said he *prikkede with powere* (rode out with an army) *his pese to disturbe* and we are referred back to the herald's discussion of treason at lines 126ff. If Shareshull's name is invoked as a hated figure of authority in this context, this in turn affects our view of Wastoure, and we recall the further equation of Wastoures with vagrants, robbers, and itinerant labourers, the usage exploited by Langland. In his edition of the C-text of *Piers Plowman* Pearsall points out that these men were frequently mentioned in Parliament and Statutes were promulgated against them in 1331, 1376, and 1383 (note to VIII. 149, p. 152).

**itwiste:** *It* and *wiste* appear as separate words in the manuscript but *itwiste*, a form of *MED itwix* 'among, between (them)' gives better sense. It is more likely that Wastoure hopes for Shareshull's downfall than that he might be discomfited by the loss of his colleagues.

321. Between *I* and *it* are caret marks (// //) directing the reader to take in from the margin, where the reading is *se*. Above the marks in the line are two further letters which appear to be *es*. It is possible that another, later hand is responsible for the redundant *es* above the line which, as it stands, reads: *For nowe I se es it es full sothe*, and all editors agree in reading *I se it es full sothe*. Gollancz also excises *full* on metrical grounds, regarding it as caught from the second half of the line.

326. **this wrechide Wastoure:** usually regarded as an error caught from *this wrechede Wynnere* in line 324. Here we are faced with the fine line between repetition as a conscious stylistic device or the result of a copyist's error, a problem discussed by Mary Hamel in her edition of *MorteArthure* (New York, 1984), pp. 15–18. In this instance the poet repeats the phrase, thus condemning the disputants as equally contemptible. For a contrary view, however, see N. Jacobs, 'The Typology of Debate and the Interpretation of *Wynnere and Wastoure*', *RES*, n.s. xxxvi (1985), p. 491, n. 55.

329. **owthe:** Manuscript *owthe* is a unique instance in the poem of a Southern inflection for the present plural, and although there are sufficient Southern forms in the text to suggest the reading is original, it may still be a copyist's error, either influenced by *fayth* and *dayntethes* below or resulting from genuine misunderstanding of the shifting syntax of lines 327–9.

330ff. By any standards, Wastoure's feast is extravagant, surpassing most examples of this form of rhetorical 'descriptio'. The king's feast in the alliterative *MorteArthure* similarly becomes a 'display of magnificence' and 'a visible sign of political and moral power' (H. Harder, 'Feasting in the Alliterative *MorteArthure*', *SMC* xiv (1980), 46–92, 156–7).

330. **he:** Second and third person pronouns alternate in this speech, and Gollancz pulls them all into the third person. The variation might represent the poet's attempt at a dramatic scene if we envisage Wynnere turning alternately to the king and to Wastoure.

332. **plontes:** Gollancz offers the attractive conjecture *bayes* where emendation cannot be successfully defended. *Plontes* is an acceptable example of voiced and unvoiced alliteration with *bores* and *broghte* forming a couplet with the following line.

336. **chewettes:** The *chewettes* have puzzled etymologists, although *MED* proposes an Anglo-Norman origin and confirms the sense 'meat, fish pies', from *The Forme of Cury*. In their recent edition of this text Constance Hieatt and Sharon Butler suggest the word 'probably means "little cabbages" (*choux*, used for modern pastries), indicating that they are small and round' (EETS, ss 8 (1985), p. 178).

**charbinade fewlis:** The manuscript's *charbiande* is more likely a scribal error than a compound of *char* OF 'flesh' and *viande* 'meat' (so *MED*), although the phrase clearly denotes some kind of meat dish. A copyist has incorrectly expanded a suspension sign for *n* in an unfamiliar word; an original *charbinade* would be an otherwise unrecorded borrowing from Old French *charbonade* 'viande rôtie à la hâte sur des charbons' (Godefroy). We may compare the sixteenth-century English noun *carbonado*. In the present context, *charbinade fewlis* may be an adjectival phrase 'grilled birds' or two nouns in apposition, 'grilled meat, birds', but the falling cadence of the line suggests the former reading.

337. **dole:** Manuscript *doke* is rejected here for the first time as an error for *dole* 'share, portion'. Although *doke* would seem to be confirmed by the context, this line serves as the general complaint Wynnere makes after itemizing the dishes for each of Wastoure's three courses (compare lines 341–3, 358–9). Wynnere's accusation is more shocking if each man is said to have a sufficient share (of boar, bucks, venison, pheasants, etc.) for six men, rather than duck enough. Confusion of *l* and *k* has marred the text elsewhere (compare lines 164, *balle* and 502 *kayre*) while the form *doke* would differ substantially from a less ambiguous reading in line 97, *drakes and . . . dukkes*.

345. **Martynmesse mete:** beef salted at Martinmas, in November.

348–52. **he, hym:** See note to line 330 above.

353–9. Folio 181, the last paper leaf in the volume as it now stands, has suffered considerable damage, in the form of general discolouring and fading and the loss of a small piece from the top left-hand corner. Affected are the beginning of lines 353–60, the end of line 468a, and the end of lines 469–73. When Gollancz made his first transcription from the manuscript, the damaged edges were covered with a small piece of paper which was later lifted to enable him to read those fragments of text previously concealed. Since the manuscript was repaired and guarded in 1972, in some lines we are now able to read a greater portion of the defective words, but conversely, the binder's restoration has sometimes obscured an earlier reading (although rarely is more than one letter affected). The British Library's microfilm, made in 1968, has been used to confirm earlier transcriptions from the manuscript, and attention is drawn to these readings in the following notes. There is nevertheless considerable variation between the transcriptions of different editors, and the manuscript's previously tight binding may have inhibited the full recovery of the text.

353. **Caudils:** 'soups, stews'. It is difficult to improve on Gollancz's conjecture from manuscript *-ils*.

354. **Dariols:** Gollancz proposed the excellent reading *dariols* 'pastries, custards' when he could read only *-ls* on the leaf. While it is now possible to read *-oils*, no other reading seems to fit the context, and I have assumed that the scribe was attracted to the final letters of [*caud*]*ils* in the preceding line.

**355. Mawmene:** Gollancz's conjecture from *-mene* has been accepted by all editors.

**356. Iche a mese:** Gollancz copied incorrectly what he saw and read *-e mese*, leading to his reconstruction, *Twelue mese at a merke* 'twelve courses at one place'. But Burrow reads correctly *-e a mese* from the manuscript and completes the line by reading *Iche a mese at a merke*, 'Each course costs a mark'. *Merke* is not recorded with Gollancz's sense 'place-setting', while Wynnere's complaint about the cost seems characteristic: a mark was worth two-thirds of a pound; *MED Mark(e)* n.(2).

The syncopation of stress and alliteration on *bytwen twa men* highlights *twa* and confirms Wynnere's tone of indignation. This variation on the normal pattern, which could be classified aa/xa or aa/bba, is also supported by the couplet alliteration on *m* with the preceding line.

**357. þat sothe bot brynneth:** A previous repair may have obscured part of the manuscript, since early editors were able to see only *-he*, where the letters *-othe* are now clearly visible. Consequently all previous conjectures (*Thanne*; *Thoghe*; *Whiche*; *þat the*) are obsolete. We may translate lines 356–7 thus: 'Each course for two men costs a mark, which surely only fires your bowels in misery'.

**358. Me tenyth:** The fragment now visible, *-enyth*, confirms Gollancz's earlier conjecture *me tenyth* from the reading *-yth*.

**359. þat iche a gome:** Again, Gollancz's conjecture from manuscript *-he a gome* is persuasive.

**362. schathed:** While the poem witnesses no other example of *sch/sk* alliteration, neither *sch* nor *sc/sk* forms an exclusive alliterating consonantal group, and the line is best read as alliterating on *s*. Cf. *Cleanness* 600, *And þat watz schewed schortly by a scaþe onez* (ed. J. J. Anderson (Manchester, 1977)).

**364. ones:** The scribe has simply omitted the final letter (compare similar errors at lines 64, 190). He may have interpreted the phrase to mean 'one man', but the line demands the sense 'one time'.

**366. forthe:** Most editions correct this reading to *forther*, thus matching the call for drinks at line 216, but the poet is not compelled to use an identical phrase to conclude each fitt and the variation may well be original. Perhaps the narrator's call for wine is placed to undercut Wastoure's pithy proverb at line 365, '*Better were meles many þan a mery nyghte*'.

**369. lite ȝeris:** While recent editors preserve the manuscript reading, *within fewe ȝeris*, the aa/xx alliteration of the line fulfils none of the usual requirements and no defence of the reading can be made on stylistic grounds. In line with the metrical policy of this edition *fewe* is emended to *lite*, and it is assumed that Thornton's reading is an unconscious use of a common formula.

**370–4.** These lines have been rejected by many editors for their failure to satisfy the demands of modern English syntax. As they stand, their chief defect is the apparent absence of a subject for *Schal* in line 373. Gollancz alters

*Thurgh* in line 370 to *Then.* Burrow's identification of a 'shift of syntax' allows us to accept the *poure plenté of corne* as the subject of *Schal.*

Line 372, *Ay to appaire þe pris and passe nott to hye* in the manuscript, also presents a syntactic difficulty which Gollancz resolves by substituting *þat it* for *and*, while Burrow reads simply *and* [*it*] *passe nott to hye*, a lighter, more elegant correction which is adopted here.

373. **in erthe:** While this phrase may be simply a tag 'on earth, in the world', Burrow suggests the possibility of word-play on 'earth' and the well attested sense of *erthe* 'ploughing' (*MED erthe* n.(2); OE *yrþ*).

386. **ichone ete oþer:** Kölbing, Schumacher, and Gollancz contend the original reading was *ichone* [*fr*] *ete oþer*, while Stern, Rosenfield, Burrow, and Turville-Petre retain the manuscript reading. As it stands, the line alliterates on the complex pattern aaa/bb with vocalic alliteration in the second half line (see Introduction).

390. **moste:** The second half of the line reads *a wastoure he fynde* with caret marks inserted after *wastoure.* In the margin we read the meaningless *moþe*, which Gollancz and Stern transcribe *moste.* This appears to be written in a different hand or at least with a different pen, but the proverbial expression clearly demands an emphatic modal auxiliary, so that whatever we make of *moþe*, the correct reading would appear to be *moste.*

**wele:** Here, and at line 496 below, the poet puns on the adverb 'well', and the noun 'wealth, prosperity'.

395. **lesse þat ʒe wrethe ʒour wifes:** the copyist seems to have confused abbreviations for *þ¹* and *7. MED* offers no instance of the phrase *lesse and.*

396. **a wale tyme:** ME *wale* adj. is usually traced to ON *val* n. 'choice, the act of choosing' and glossed 'fine, choice, good'. But Gollancz derives *wale* from East Frisian *wale* 'turn around', used to suggest a brief period of time or time passing quickly. This would be an appropriate sense here as Wastoure sells off his timber for a quick financial return. The sense 'pleasant' is impossible in the lines Gollancz quotes from *The Wars of Alexander*: *þare suld my folk for defaute be famyscht for euire, / And worthe in a wale quile to wricchis as ʒour-selfe!* (ed. W. W. Skeat, EETS, ES 47 (1886), ll. 4596–7).

400. **schadewe:** *Saue to* is emended to *schadewe* on grammatical and stylistic rather than alliterative grounds. Alliteration on *s* or *sch* would form a couplet with the following line but the manuscript's sense is poor and repetitive. We have already been told that Wastoure will *spare* the seedlings and saplings for his children, and *saue* in line 400 was probably caught from *saue ʒe þe soyle* immediately below. Gollancz's attractive emendation to *schadewe* 'provide shade for' is adopted by most editors.

405. **brod launde:** A large ink blot covers the space between *brod* and *launde*; Gollancz and Burrow both read *brode.*

407. Wynnere's concern for the dissipation of Wastoure's inheritance recalls a legal sense of the noun *waste*, as 'Any unauthorised act of a tenant for

a freehold estate not of inheritance, or for any lesser interest, which tends to the destruction of the tenement, or otherwise to the injury of the inheritance' (Pollock, *Law of Torts*, 1887, p. 255, *OED Waste sb.*⁷). See also D. V. Moran, '*Wynnere and Wastoure*: An Extended Footnote', *NM* lxxiii (1972), 683–5.

**408. Wasted:** One of the few instances where the tense found in manuscript *Wastes* cannot easily be defended, this phrase plainly forms a parallel with the previous line, *Now es it sett and solde.* The simple emendation of *wastes* to *wasted* proposed by Kölbing easily corrects an error induced either by *es* in line 407, or by the inflections of the several plural nouns in the following lines. Alternatively, Thornton's exemplar may have used an unfamiliar abbreviation for *es*, a contraction he himself used only twice in this text.

**409. That are had ben lordes:** Lines 409–15 have probably suffered greater scribal corruption than we can trace in the manuscript, and their sense is correspondingly elusive. The first problem of interpretation arises with those *nysottes* who are now followers of fashion *That are had lordes in londe and ladyes riche.* Gollancz retains the manuscript reading and compares these lines to fourteenth-century estates satire, taking the subject to be servants 'who formerly (*are*) had lords . . .' and who are now commanding higher wages and imitating their social superiors. But the context of Wynnere's argument suggests a reference to members of the nobility who are now squandering their heritage on the fleeting pleasures of high fashion. This would follow Wynnere's comparison between Wastoure and his ancestors at lines 402–8 and anticipate the later contrast between the rich *nysottes* and the poor girls *þat neuer silke wroghte*, although as Burrow comments, this comparison is less than enlightening and the passage may yet be corrupt.

If we take line 409 to refer to *lordes and ladyes*, the manuscript reading, *That are had lordes . . .* is weak. Burrow glosses *had* 'considered, held' yet Kölbing's correction to *That are had [ben] lordes . . .* may be preferable. Scribal confusion over this difficult passage and the resemblance of *are* 'formerly' to a part of the verb 'to be' could easily account for the omission, while the imperfect state of the passage probably represents Thornton's efforts to correct a corrupt exemplar.

**411. syde slabbande sleues:** The manuscript's *elde slabbande sleues* makes poor sense and most editors adopt Gollancz's emendation to *side* or *syde* 'wide', a conjecture which finds support in venality satire, where the trailing sleeves of fourteenth-century fashion are a common butt of the satirist's humour and the homilist's condemnation. See *Mum and the Sothsegger* III. 152–3, 234 and the Harley lyric, 'In a fryht as y con fare fremede': *Betere is were þunne boute laste / þen syde robes ant synke into synne* (15–16). This conjectural reading is more persuasive than Turville-Petre's *sleghe* 'skilfully made'. Wynnere has no reason to praise the workmanship in these garments while he is naturally concerned about vanity, waste, and extravagance. *Syde slabbande sleues* are strictly tappets that hung from above the elbow, with a slit on the inside, often so long that they trailed on the ground in the mud (cf. Chaucer's *Parson's Tale*, 418–19).

415. **lyre:** Burrow defends *lyre* persuasively as 'misfortune, hardship' (s.v. *MED lire* n.(1), 3(b), from OE *lyre*). Gollancz had imagined an elaborate sequence of error from an original *whoso lykes luke on hir*, but Burrow's reading is confirmed by the description of Mary's hardship in the following lines.

419. **þat hend:** the sole use of the absolute adjective in the poem, a grammatical construction which is often regarded as a distinctive feature of alliterative poetry.

420. **wedes:** Scribal anticipation of *pore* accounts for manuscript *wordes*. Gollancz's correction to *wedes* restores good sense.

422. **þat pouerte ofte schewes:** either a parenthetical comment on the preceding lines or a clause directly relative to them. Gollancz opts for the second alternative and adjusts the text: *þat pouerte* [*e*]*schewes* '(to abandon the ostentation and display) that poverty avoids'. Burrow preserves the manuscript reading as an independent clause—'poverty often demonstrates this', but it is better read as a relative clause, 'which poverty often teaches'. Gollancz's excision of *For* at the beginning of the line is also unnecessary.

423. **castes:** The manuscript line gives aa/xx alliteration but couplet alliteration with line 424 seems to be sufficient compensation for the incomplete alliteration, even though, elsewhere, we have insisted on alliteration between voiced and unvoiced sounds in this situation. There are no grounds for suspecting scribal interference, however, and the phrase is stylistically strong.

429. **faire chere:** This line alliterates ax/ax, a pattern accepted at line 132 above and supplemented here by the alliterative link with *fynde* in the preceding line. *Chere* is used rather loosely none the less for 'demeanour, mood, humour' or 'sympathy (shown to the lover)', and the line is difficult to translate, particularly as *to forthir hir herte* appears to be a common phrase meaning simply 'to please her' (cf. line 464). The basic sense is clear: Wastoure's *lede* must provide for his mistress so as to please her and win her good opinion of him. In this passage Wastoure closely resembles ʒouthe in *The Parlement of the Thre Ages* (cf. lines 246–60) but the courtly, heroic vocabulary (*birdes*, *lemman*, *schalkes*) and conservative tone ring false. We are reminded of the passage in *Piers Plowman* which has been characterized as playing on the high alliterative style, when Mede is brought to Westminster (J. A. Burrow, 'The Audience of *Piers Plowman*', *Anglia*, lxxv (1957), p. 381).

434. **see:** Gollancz first misread manuscript *fee* as *see*, and it is true that long *s* and *f* become more difficult to distinguish on the last, hurriedly written, and faded leaf. Steadman noted the error and Gollancz subsequently emended *fee* to *see*. Burrow suggests that 'the MS. reading ('enfeoff') may be right' and Turville-Petre preserves *fee* as 'reward', but *MED* translates *feen* v. more technically as 'enfeoff, hire', and this latter sense is contradicted by the expression *faire and free* (Turville-Petre glosses this as 'nobly'). Moreover, the

reference to *myn eghne* supports *see* rather than *fee*, and Gollancz's emendation is adopted here: *To [s]ee þam faire and free tofore with myn eghne*, assuming confusion of *s* and *f* in an earlier exemplar.

435–8. Wishing to make the description of Wynnere accord with the traditional portrayal of the avaricious man who cannot sleep for anxiety about his wealth, Gollancz transforms these lines completely:

> And 3e negardes, appon nyghte, nappe ' 3e ' [neuer] so harde,
> R[axill]en at 3our r[outt]yng, raysen 3our hurd[i]es;
> Beden[e] ' 3e wayte one þe wedir, þen wery 3e þe while,
> þat 3e [h]ade hightilde vp your houses & 3our hyne [a]rayed.

In this very bold treatment of the text, the passage is made to suggest Wynnere's insomnia and regret that he has spent money making improvements to his estate which were unnecessary because of poor harvests. The negative in line 438 is then changed to *hade*, and manuscript *Routten at 3our raxillyng* 'snore as you stretch' to *Raxillen at 3our routtyng*, 'Ye start 'mid your snoring'. Line 436b is glossed 'spring up on your haunches', to suggest restlessness.

On the other hand, the manuscript readings provide a more subtle contrast between Wastoure's own activity in consumption, self-improvement for the sake of his mistress, and Wynnere's slothfulness: *Forthi, Wynnere, with wronge þou wastis þi tyme.* This paradoxical accusation draws its impact from the previous lines as they stand in the manuscript. *Harde* in line 435 can mean 'soundly, firmly'; *MED harde* adv. 1(a), 2(b), (c), a sense borne out by the following description of Wynnere's snores as he stretches in his bed, raising his buttocks (surely in profound sleep rather than restlessness). In his sloth, he postpones making expensive improvements to his barns and increasing his flocks in case bad weather causes a small harvest. And when the weather stays good, he curses himself for his inability to reap and store the harvest. Wynnere is certainly accused of insomnia earlier at line 248, but the accusation of slothfulness fits this slightly different context.

**beden:** Gollancz presumes the loss of an adverb, 'ever and anon', and reads **Beden[e] 3e wayte**.... There is no reason why a form of OE *bēodan* should be inappropriate here. *3e beden wayte on þe wedir* ... thus translates 'You give orders to wait on the weather....'

442. **were:** 'keep or hold, possess', from OE *werian*, *wergan* 'use' (*OED Were v.* 2d).

445. **tast no tent:** The scribe has almost certainly omitted *no* from the line.

446–7. **make:** Gollancz rejects Wastoure's sudden change of topic and corrects *his make for to wyn* to *his makande to wyn*. Admittedly Wastoure has made a sudden and self-contradictory change in direction: instead of speaking of women in terms of an old courtly ethic he now seems to accept Wynnere's description of his behaviour in the tavern (lines 277–82). He now takes up the theme of his aggressive rejection of ancient familial tradition in favour of a short and pleasant life.

454. **hert:** The scribe's characteristic error of omission is easily corrected.

460. **wale stremys:** It is difficult to gloss *wale* accurately. Rosenfield derives the word from OE *wæl* 'dangerous, deadly', but Gollancz's sense 'swift' (see note to line 396 above) would be more fitting. Alternatively, the more familiar sense of *wale* 'fine, beautiful, pleasant' may be appropriate here.

468–73. These lines are affected by damage to the last leaf of the manuscript. While alliteration could be used as a guide to the reconstruction of lines 353ff., there are fewer guidelines where the last word or words of the lines are missing. Moreover, these lines do not appear within a catalogue but form a crucial part of the king's incomplete and cryptic summing up.

468. **come:** Line 468 is copied as two short lines and the tear in the manuscript cuts through the last word in the first half-line, leaving *co-*. The restoration to *co*[*me*] is straightforward.

469. **til þou þi lefe take:** Only the final word is missing, and Turville-Petre's conjecture *take* supplies more regular alliteration than Gollancz's *lache*.

470. **beryinge-daye:** The reading is adopted by all editors to supplement the manuscript fragment *ber-*. It may be that Gollancz's successful and attractive conjecture has blinded subsequent editors to other possibilities; it is certainly difficult to improve on the resultant text.

471. **a fote for to holde:** This line is problematic in that the portion of text remaining, *With hym happyns þe neuer a fote for . . .* may also be metrically defective. Various solutions have been proposed, including the substitution of *falles* for *happyns*, and reading *to neghe*, *to strecche*, or *to passe* at the end of the line. The difficulty may stem from an idiomatic expression inverted in the second half-line for variation or emphasis (compare the resultant aa/xa pattern at lines 197 and 356). Under *fot* n. 6(c), *MED* records the metaphorical sense 'power to stand', and several idiomatic expressions such as *cacchen fot* 'get a foothold, become established' and *geten fot* 'make headway'. *MED fot* n. 14(k) also records the phrase *holden fot* 'to keep up (with someone in walking); to stand one's ground'; this would provide excellent figurative sense if line 471 is reconstructed on the aa/xa alliterative pattern: *With hym happyns þe neuer a fote for* [*to holde*]. Even if Wynnere were to remain in London all his days, as long as Wastoure lives in the kingdom, Wynnere will never be able to establish himself.

472. **wonne scholde:** The manuscript reads *won* with one further minim stroke which would give us *wonn*, almost certainly for *wonne*, inf. 'dwell'. However, Gollancz throws the passage into confusion by reading *I will þat þou wonne þer euer*, even though we have just been told that Wastoure must leave the country when Wynnere returns. Rosenfield leaves the period of Wastoure's exile indeterminate with his conjecture *þat þou wonn*[*e scholde*], and this reading is adopted here.

473. **wyng þer vntill:** When Gollancz first consulted the manuscript, he

saw that the tear which affects these first lines of the column comes to an uneven point between *wyng* and *till*, with a fragment of what looks like *n* visible before *till*. This word is also visible on the microfilm, but must have broken away before Stern and Rosenfield consulted the manuscript, because they record only *wyng* . . ., and the leaf is now patched from *wyng* up to the extreme right-hand edge of the leaf. Fortunately, the microfilm confirms the reading *wyng* . . .*(n)till*. Gollancz takes *wyng* as part of a present indicative verb and reads *wynges vntill*. He translates 'Where is most waste of wealth and (it) easily flies away', but this seems strained. Rosenfield and Turville-Petre take *wyng* as an imperative, reading *and wyng(e) þer vntill* 'and hurry thither' (Turville-Petre). Even though *wyng* is not recorded as a verbal form until Shakespeare, this is probably the best reading of the text.

476. **petit:** The manuscript reads *Where any potet beryn þurgh þe burgh passe* and has occasioned considerable editorial speculation. Gollancz constructed an elaborate case ('positively fascinating in its subtlety', says Steadman) for *potet* as a corruption of *potener* = pautener, OF *pautonniere* 'bag, purse', arguing that the original expression was *any berande potener* 'anyone carrying a purse'. Holthausen proposed correcting the form to *bostous*, then later proposed *bold*, while others have recognized that the line is an example of double alliteration on voiced and unvoiced consonants: ab/ba. Stern reads *pert*, while Rosenfield offers *potent*, but neither of these readings offers good sense. The form is reconstructed here as *petit* 'small, insignificant, trifling', used first as an adjective by Langland, in both its early senses of 'small' and 'of little importance'. See *MED petit* adj., and *Piers Plowman* A. VIII. 59, B. XIV. 243. If Langland or the *Wynnere and Wastoure*-poet was the first to borrow the word from the French we should not be surprised if a fifteenth-century Yorkshire scribe who may not have known much French does not recognize the form. *Petit* gives excellent sense, in that Wastoure is thus instructed to seek out any insignificant man, no matter how poor, and ruin him.

Only Turville-Petre preserves the manuscript reading, with the uncertain gloss 'tippler?'

480. **bikken:** Gollancz restores the usual intransitive sense to the verb and smooths the metre by reading *bikken [with] þi fynger*. But the phrase reads like a colloquial expression and we should be reluctant to tamper with it (cf. *MED bekenen* v. and *bekken* v.).

482. **"hotte for the hungry":** this seems to be a street vendor's cry, and is punctuated accordingly. We may compare *Piers Plowman* A. Prol. 104–5 and 'London Lickpenny', lines 59ff. (R. H. Robbins, *Historical Poems*, no. 51).

484. The manuscript's absolute use of *after* in *sythen send after* in line 483 is unprecedented, and the present text assumes the accidental omission of *And* (probably in the form of an ampersand) at the beginning of the line. This might have been lost or dropped to the following line, *and luke thi knafe* . . . and

the scribe's eye may have been caught by line 480, which begins *Brynge hym to Bred Strete.*

485. **sprede:** The microfilm reads *spre*, but the manuscript has been torn and repaired with the loss of final -*e.* The incomplete word is almost certainly *sprede* (as all editors reconstruct the line) and the mark through *þ* is either accidental or ornamental.

487. **fynd a peny:** Gollancz translates 'devil a penny', but the evidence he cited for this expression dates from 1714, and the line is better read as an idiomatic construction—half imperative, half conditional: 'Find so much as one penny in his wallet . . .'.

**eghe:** This reading was confirmed from the microfilm, as the manuscript has been torn and repaired through final -*e.*

492. **þe henne wele to serue:** Gollancz reconstructs the manuscript's *þe henne wele serue* as *þe hennes wele serued*, but *henne* in the singular picks up an earlier theme which takes a hen as a familiar image: compare lines 347, 387, 482. Stern adopts Gollancz's readings but also postulates the omission of a preposition before *serue*: *to* is inserted here, making a parallel construction of *þe henne wele* [*to*] *serue* with *to knawen þi fode* in the previous line.

494. **þe endes:** The manuscript reading, *þis oþer foules*, is almost certainly a scribal substitution for an illegible or unfamiliar word, presumably the name of another bird. *Foules* is an uncharacteristic spelling (compare *few(l)lys* at lines 44, 91, 96, 336, 384, but the presumably scribal *foles* at line 40). Gollancz reads *þe osulles* yet while this word appears in many variant forms, it is not in itself rare. Another possibility might be *endes* 'ducks'. From OE *ened* and Latin *anat-em*, the word appears in *The Parlement of the Thre Ages* line 220 (see Offord's note) and in *Havelok the Dane*: *Ne was þer spared gos ne henne / Ne þe ende, ne the drake / Mete he deden plente make: / Ne wantede þere no god mete* (1240–3) (ed. W. W. Skeat, 2nd edn, rev. K. Sisam, Oxford, 1915). The word is sufficiently rare to be misunderstood (the Laud manuscript scribe of *Havelok* spells the word *hende*), and a copyist unfamiliar with the word might have construed it as 'end', and deliberately corrected this apparent error.

500. **siluer:** Although all editors agree in reading *siluer*, the manuscript has suffered further damage since Gollancz first examined the text. The leaf is intact, but the reading is blurred and faded, although not 'rubbed out' as Gollancz has it. It is now possible to make out *sil*, although only the bottom of *l* is still visible.

502. **kayre:** The manuscript reads *layren*, although Gollancz transcribes the form as *kayren* without comment, glossing the form as an infinitive (although cf. *cayre* inf. 240, 468). Yet it is awkward and confusing for the king to say *I thynk to . . . kayren as I come.*

The king is clearly giving Wynnere a further instruction, bidding him join his other followers; *kayren* is probably an error for *kayre* in the imperative singular, forming a parallel with the long sequence of injunctions and directions to each disputant which forms the king's summing-up. The correction is a simple and uncontroversial one; the scribe may have added final *-n* after writing the nasal suspension sign of *sythen*, or by inducement from *foloen* and *lufen*. We have considerable evidence that this portion of the text was copied in haste, and the scribe's undoubted misreading of the initial letter alerts our suspicions to the possibility of further corruption.

# GLOSSARY

The Glossary records all forms, though not all occurrences of each form in the emended text. Verbal forms are listed under their infinitives, if these occur in the text, or present indicative forms, since in a mixed dialect to predict an infinitive form can be misleading. An asterisk (*) beside a head-word or a line number indicates that the form in the text is conjectural and *n.* following a line number refers the reader to a discussion of the word's origin, sense, or form in the Commentary. Personal names and place-names are listed separately.

In the glossary, ʒ is placed after *g* and þ is included with *th* under *t. Y* is not used to represent a consonant in this text and is treated throughout as *i.* Initial *u* and *v* are distinguished only in so far as they represent a vowel or a consonant.

Most abbreviations used will be obvious. Others are as follows: her., heraldic; leg., legal; AN, Anglo-Norman; Du., Dutch; EFris., East Frisian; Icel., Icelandic; M. Sw., Middle Swedish; MLG, Middle Low German; MnE, Modern English; OE, Old English (West Saxon); OF, Old French; ON, Old Norse; Sc., Scots; Scand., Scandinavian; and Sw. Swedish.

## A

**a** *indef. art.* a 10, 24, 26; one 365; **an(e)** (before vowels or **h**) 36, 50, 70, but **a hen** 482.

**aboute, abowte** *adv.* around, all over, about 249, 280, 412; in all directions 443.

**aftir(e)** *adv.* afterwards 16, 133, 291, behind 207; **after, aftir** *prep.* after 303, 305, 396; for (**hope, send, trotte ~**) 290, 483, 489; for the sake of 429.

**agayne** *prep.* against 172.

**age** *n.* age, time of life 120.

**ay(e)** *adv.* ever 372; ~ **when** whenever 227.

**ayther(e)** *adj.* either, each 50, 58, 202.

**albus** *n.pl.* bullfinches 494 [unkn. cf. MnE dial. *blood-alp*].

**al(le)** *adj.* all 67, 138, 162; **all(e)** *pron.* all, everything, everyone 5, 55, 159; **all(e)** *adv.* entirely, very, quite 60, 71, 75; *with conj.* ~ þofe although 420.

**a(l)s** *conj.* as, when, while 32, 45, 85; as if 343; *adv.* as, like, just as 4, 26, 71, 125.

**amblande** *pr.p.adj.* walking, ambling 417.

**amonges** *prep.* amongst 136.

**and** *conj.* and 1, 5, 6; if 259.

**angarte** *adj.* excessive, immoderate 267n.

**any** *adj.* any 56, 68, 120; *adv.* 216.

**anone** *adv.* immediately 214.

**anoþer, anothir** *adj.* another 149, 469; *pron.* 116, 338, 391.

**appaire** *inf.* lower, lessen 372.

**appon(e), vpon** *prep.* on, upon 13, 51, 58; in 24, 66, 67; to, into 497; at 11, 306, 435; ~ **lofte** above, on top 72, 163, 184.

**are** *conj.* before 198, 269; *adv.* 409n.

**are(n)** see **be(n)**

**armes** *n.pl.* weapons; **men of** ~ soldiers 193.

**as** see **als**

**askes** *3 sg.pr.* orders 213.

**assche** *n.* ash-tree 397.

**asse** *n.* donkey, ass 417.

**at** *prep.* at 15, 29, 45; on 59.

**attyred(e)** *p.p.adj.* attired, decked out 203, 270, 410.

**aughte** see **ogh**

**awaye** *adv.* gone, away 183n., 283.

## B

**bachelere** *n.* knight (in another's service) 328.

**bacon, bakone** *n.* bacon 251, 379.

**baken** *p.p.adj.* roasted 335.

**bakke** *n.* at þe ~, þi ~, behind 114, 116, 307.

**bale** *n.* pain 357.

**bale** *adj.* terrible, wicked 292.

**balle*** *n.* sphere 164.

**baner(e)** *n.* banner 143, 149, 156; company of armed men 131, 168; **baners** pl. 52.

**bankes** see **bonke**

**bare** see **bere**

**barkes** *n.pl.* husks, shells 39n.

**barme** *n.* lap, breast 418.

**barne** *n.* child 418.

**barone** *n.* lord, noble 328.

**barnakes** *n.pl.* wild geese 349. [L *berneca*; OF *bernaque*]

**batell** *n.* conflict, battle 105.

**be, bi, by** *prep.* by 4, 49, beside 33, 34, 83; through 125; according to 176; along 340.

**bede-hede** *n.* the head of a bed 239.

**beden** *2 pl.pr.* give orders 437n. [OE *bēodan*]

**beefe** *n.* beef 379.

**before, byfore** *adv.* in advance, ahead 207; formerly 272; ~ **and behynde** (her.) above and below 78n.; *prep.* before, in front of 228, 277.

**begynnes** *3 sg.pr.* begins *incipit*.

**behynde, byhynde** *adv.* behind, at the back 76, below 78 (see **before**); **holden** ~ remain at home 9n.

**belyue** *adv.* quickly, immediately 46.

**belte** *n.* girdle, belt 96, 187; **beltys** *pl.* 182.

**bemys** *n.pl.* beams 251.

**be(n)** *inf.* to be 27, 201, 255; remain 388; **let** ~ cease 255; **es** *3 sg.pr.* 5, 18, 21; **are** *2 pl.pr.* 362; *3 pl.* 142, 152, 159; **aren** 160, 219, 234; **ben(e)** *3 pl.pr.* 12, 29, 235; **be** *3 sg.pr.subj.* 126, 131, 147; **ben** *3 pl.pr.subj.* 433; **was** *1 sg.pa.* 46, 47, 85; *3 sg.* 1, 10, 33; **wer(e)** *3 pl.* 19, 22, 42; *3 sg.pa.subj.* 308, 338, 343; *3 pl.pa.subj.* 98, 312, 313; **ben(e)** *p.p.* 3, 409*.

**bende** *n.* (her.) broad diagonal band 149.

**benden** *3 pl.pr.* bend, twist 251.

**bent** *n.* field, battlefield 105, 143, 156.

**bere** *inf.* bear, carry 30; **bare** *3 sg.pa.* 93; **borne** *p.p.* 307.

**bery-brown** *adj.* brown as a berry 91.

**beryinge-daye**\* *n.* burying day 470.

**beryn(e)** *n.* knight, nobleman 101, 168, 328; man 126, 131; servant 278; in direct address, sir, man 307; **beryns** *pl.* 457; servants 214; judges, lords 314.

**bernacles** *n.pl.* wild geese 39. [OF *bernacle*, L *bernacula*]

**besantes** *n.pl.* gold ornaments resembling coins 61.

**besyde** *adv.* moreover, in addition 138, 170; *prep.* next to, alongside 36, 333.

**beste** *n.* beast, animal 73; **bestes, bestis** *pl.* 79, 385.

**betyde** see **bytyde**

**betyn** *p.p.adj.* stamped, beaten 61.

**by** *inf.* pay for 393, 425.

**by** *prep.* see **be**

**bid** *1 sg.pr.* ask, bid 197; **biddes** *3 sg.pr.* 239, **biddith** 101; **bidd** *imper.sg.* 105.

**bide** *2 sg.pr.subj.* remain 470.

**byfore** see **before**

**biggede** *p.p.* settled, founded 1.

**byhynde** see **behynde**

**bikken** *imper.sg.* point, beckon 480n.

**billes** *n.pl.* bills, beaks 39; **billed** *adj.* beaked 349.

**bynche** *n.* wide throne 87; **bynches** *pl.* judicial benches 314.

**birdes, byrddes** *n.pl.*[1] fowls 348, 493. [OE *bridd*]

**birdes** *n.pl.*[2] ladies 426. [OE *(ge)byrd*]

**birre** *n.* violent blast, **at a** ~ instantly 292.

**bytyde** *3 sg.pa.* happened 31; **betyde** *3 sg.pr.subj.* 204.

**bytwen(e)** *adv.* between 65; *prep.* 41, 54, 219.

**bytwixe** *prep.* between *incipit*.

**blake** *n.* black 182, (her.) sable 143, 164.

**blasande** *pr.p.adj.* blazing 342; **blesenande** splendid, illustrious 168.

**bleaunt**\* *n.* stuff, material 91.

**ble(e)** *n.* colour 93, 96, 144.

**blerren** *inf.* dim, blur the vision, ~ **eghne** 278.

**blewe** *adj.* blue, (her.) azure 93.

**blynnes** *imper.pl.* cease 457.

**blode** *n.* spirit, **of** ~ spirited 14, 194.

**blussche** *n.* gleam 187.

**bocled, buklede** *p.p.adj.* buckled, fastened 114, 182.

**body** *n.* body 114.

**boyes** *n.pl.* commoners, men of low birth 14.

**bokels** *n.pl.* buckles 158.

**bolde** *adj.* bold, daring 105, 126, 131; confident, fearless 194, 431.

**bolle** *n.* drinking bowl, cup 278; **bolles** *pl.* 214.

**bone** *n.* ivory 181, **bones** *pl.* limbs 111.

**bonets**\* *n.pl.* coifs, hoods 314n.

**bonke** *n.* bank, slope 33, 109; **bankes** *pl.* 41.

**borde, burde** *n.* table 335, 342.

**bore** *n.* wild boar, ~ **hedis** 175; **bores** *gen.sg.* 332.

**boste** *n.* presumption, arrogance 14.

**boste** *inf.* strut, threaten 241.

**bot** *conj.* but, however, yet 4, 17, 21; only 54, 357, **bott** 281; unless 485.

**bothe(n)** *adj.* both 123, 126, 164; *adv.* 397.

**botours, buturs** *n.pl.* bitterns 349, 379.

**bourne** *n.* stream, river 33, 41.

**bowells** *n.pl.* intestines 357.

**bowmen** *n.pl.* archers 194.

**bowndes** *n.pl.* bands, hoops 252.

**bown(n)** *adj.* ready, prepared 52, 110, 208.

**brayde** *v.* ~ **vp,** ~ **owte,** raise, flourish; **brayde\*** *3 sg.pa.* 121, **brayden** *3 pl.pa.* 52, **brayde** *p.p.* 163; **brauden, brouden** *p.p.adj.* linked, embroidered 113, 144. See also **brouderde.**

**brake** *3 sg.pa.* broke 121; **broken** *p.p.adj.* 418.

**brande, bronde** *n.* sword 239, 241; **brandes** *pl.* 431.

**brase** *n.* strap 158; **brases** *pl.* pieces of armour covering the arms 113.

**braunche** *n.* branch 121.

**braundesche** *inf.refl.* strut 241.

**bremly** *adv.* loudly, vigorously 41.

**brene** *inf.* burn 292; **brynneth** *3 sg.pr.* stings 357.

**brerdes** *n.pl.* borders, (her.) bordures 164.

**breste** *n.* breast *or* breastplate 116.

**brethe** *n.* anger 457. [ON *brǽði*]

**brydells** *n.pl.* bridles 208.

**bright(e), bryghte** *adj.* brilliant, shining 33, 50, 61; vivid, gay 96, 175, 426.

**bryng** *inf.* bring 405; **broghte** *3 pl.pa.* 197, 214; **bryng(e)** *imper.sg.* 480, 484; **broghte** *p.p.* 332.

**brynneth** see **brene**

**broche** *n.* skewer, spit 348.

**brod(e)** *adj.* wide, ample 116, 333; spacious 405; bold, uninhibited 457.

**broken** see **brake**

**bronde** see **brande**

**brothes** *n.pl.* soups, sauces 333.

**brothir** *n.* brother, partner 309.

**brouden** see **brayde**

**brouderde, broudirde** *p.p.adj.* embroidered 91, 96

**broun, brown** *adj.* shining 113, brown 158; see also **bery-brown.**

**bukkes** *n.pl.* male deer 405; **buktayles** *pl.* hindquarters of bucks 333.

**bulles\*** *n.pl.* Papal bulls 144.

**burde** see **borde**

**burgh** *n.* town, city 470, 476, 484.

**busked** *p.p.* prepared 110.

**buturs** see **botours**

## C

**caban(e)** *n.* tent, pavilion 59, 83.

**cache** *inf.* gather, harvest 274.

**cayre** *inf.* ride, go 240, 468; **kayren** *3 pl.pr.* 210; **kayre\*** *imper.sg.* 502.

**caytef(fe)** *n.* wretch, scoundrel 233, 425.

**calles** *3 pl.pr.* name, call 242.

**can(e), kan(e)** *1 sg.pr.* know, know how to 176, 223, 452; *3 sg.pr.* 26, 30, 192; **couthe** *3 pl.pa.* 20; *1 sg.subj.pa.* 308.

**capill** *n.* horse, gelding 240.

**cardynalls** *n.pl.* cardinals 462.

**care** *n.* concern 233.

**carpe** *inf.* speak 452; **kerpede** *3 sg.pa.* 218.

**case** *n.* case (leg.) 319; **þe** ~ chance 448.

**castes** *3 sg.pr.* throws, raises 423; **casten** *p.p.* divided 77.

**caudils\*** *n.pl.* soups, stews 353.

**cely** *adj.* poor, innocent 414

**certys** *adv.* certainly 221.

**chambre** *n.* apartment, room 474.

**charbinade\*** *adj.* grilled 336n.

**chechun** *n.* escutcheon, coat of arms 116n.

**chefe** *inf.* thrive, prosper 496.

**chepe** *n.*[1] sheep 481. [OE *scēap*]

**chepe** *n.*[2] market, Cheapside 474. [OE *cēap*]

**chere** *n.* face 24; cheer, happiness 383; friendliness, sympathy 429n.

**chese** *imper.sg.refl.* ~ **þe** betake yourself 474.

**chewettes** *n.pl.* meat pies 336n.

**childe** *n.* youth, lad 24; **children** *pl.* offspring, descendants 398.

**chyn-wedys** *n.pl.* facial hair, beard 24.

**choppede** *p.p.adj.* minced, diced 336.

**clene** *adj.* bright, shining 81; bare, clean 486; *adv.* brightly, splendidly 112.

**clenly** *adv.* neatly, skilfully 77.

**clepen** *3 pl.pr.* call, name 355.

**clerke** *n.* scholar 293; **clerkes** *pl.* 315.

**clyffe** *n.* hill, cliff 59, 210.

**clothe** *n.* tablecloth 485; **clothes** *pl.* garments 425.

**clothes** *3 sg.pr.* provides with clothes 205; **clade** *p.p.* dressed 90.

**clouen** *p.p.adj.* split 340.

**cofers** *n.pl.* chests, trunks 298.
**colde** *adj.* chilly, cold 275; *as n.* coldness 293.
**come** *inf.* come, arrive 293, 468*; *1 sg.pr.* 502; **comes** *3 sg.pr.* 338, comes around 448; **come** *3 sg.pa.subj.* 55, 253, 402.
**com(e)ly, comliche** *adj.* noble, handsome 86, 199, 203; **comliche** *adv.* splendidly, beautifully 90.
**comforth** *inf.* strengthen, invigorate 479.
**connynges** *n.pl.* rabbits 353.
**coppe** *n.* bowl, cup, (fig.) chance 448.
**corde** *n.* braid, cord 145.
**corne** *n.* cereal, corn 233, 370; **cornes** *pl.* 274.
**cornere** *n.* corner, quarter of an escutcheon 81.
**coste** *3 pl.pa.* cost 271, 354; *p.p.* 425.
**coursers** *n.pl.* chargers, war-horses 203.
**couthe** see **cane**
**crafte** *n.* knowledge, skill 176.
**craftyly** *adv.* cleverly, artfully 151.
**cramynge** *vbl.n.* stuffing 255.
**creste** *n.* summit, crest 59; **crestys** *pl.* crests of helmets 51.
**crete** *n.* sweet wine 479.
**croked** *p.p.adj.* curled 151.
**crowned** *p.p.adj.* crowned, wearing a crown 86.
**custadis** *n.pl.* open pies, flans 353. [AN *\*crustade*, cf. *cruste*]
**cuttede** *p.p.adj.* gelded 240.

### D

**daderande** *pr.p.adj.* trembling 97.
**dadillyng** *vbl.n.* tumult, twittering 44n.
**day(e)** *n.* day 153, 167, 220; lifetime 303, 305; **dayes** *pl.* 310.
**dayntethes** *n.pl.* delicacies 330.
**dale** *n.* donation, alms 305; **maken ~** give alms or gifts 303.
**dare** *3 sg.pr.* cares, ventures 7; **durste** *2 sg.pa.* 303.
**dariols*** *n.pl.* pastries, pies 354.
**ded** *n.* **dedis** *pl.* actions, conduct 292; **in ~** in fact, assuredly 499.
**dede, dethe** *n.* death 196, 313.
**dede** *adj.* barren 276.
**dede-day** *n.* time of death 441.
**dedly** *adj.* mortal; **~ synn** 313.
**dele** *n.* part 4.
**dele, delyn** *inf.* divide, distribute 441; deliver (blows) 142; *intr.* fight 103, 153,

167; **with ~** *inf.* concern oneself with 345; **with ~** *1 pl.pr.* 5.
**deme** *inf.* judge, arbitrate 220, 458; *imper.sg.* 244, 453; **demeth*** *3 sg.pr.* 201.
**depe** *adj.* deep 44, 312.
**dere** *adj.* expensive 494; *adv.* dearly 354.
**derne** *n.* darkness 413.
**dethe** see **dede** *n.*
**deuyll** *n.* devil 441; **the ~ wounder*** a great marvel 236n.
**dighte** *inf.* summon 330.
**dyn** *n.* loud noise 44.
**dyne** *inf.* eat, dine 330.
**dynttis** *n.pl.* blows, strokes 103, 153, 167.
**dische-metis** *n.pl.* pies, flans 354.
**disches** *n.pl.* plates, dishes 342.
**dist(o)urbe** *inf.* interrupt, disturb 129, 318.
**do** *inf.* do, perform an action, avail, make, finish; **do** *inf.* 499; **dose** *3 sg.pr.* 305; **dide** *3 sg.pa.* 451; **doo** *imper.sg.* 478; **dothe** *imper.pl.* 220; **don(e)** *p.p.* 290, 488; **dothe hym doun** *3 sg.pr.* comes down 109.
**dole*** *n.* share, portion 337. [OE *dāl*]
**domesday** *n.* day of judgement 16.
**doun, downn** *adv.* down 109, 209; in ruins, destruction 12, 235.
**dowfehowses** *n.pl.* dovecotes 235.
**drakes** *n.pl.* drakes 97.
**draweth** *3 sg.pr.* approaches 16.
**drede** *inf.* become frightened 322.
**dredfull** *adj.* awesome 16.
**dry(e)** *adj.* evaporated, parched 235; thirsty 478; *as n.* drought 276.
**drightyns** *n.gen.sg.* the Lord's 244.
**drynke** *inf.* drink 478; **dronken** *p.p.* spent on wine or ale 488.
**droghte** *n.* dryness, drought 312.
**dropeles** *adj.* rainless, dry 276.
**drownede** *p.p.* drowned 312.
**dub** *inf.* make (one) a knight 499; **dubbede** *1 sg.pa.* 103.
**duell(e)** *inf.* live, reside 453, 458; **dwellys** *3 sg.pr.* tarries 109; **duellen** *3 pl.pr.* 140; **duell** *imper.sg.* 488.
**dukkes** *n.pl.* ducks 97.
**dures** *3 sg.pr.* lasts 108.

### E

**eghe** *n.* eye 487; **eghne** *pl.* 45, 89, 126.
**egretes** *n.pl.* egrets 494.
**eke** *adv.* also, likewise 14, 310.
**eldes** *3 sg.pr.* grows old 9. [OE *ealdian*]

**ells** *adj.* other 56.

**ende** *n.* part of a country 47; end of a period of time 262, 387.

**endes*** *n.pl.* ducks 494n.

**endes** *3 sg.pr.* ends, finishes 217, 367.

**endityde** *p.p.* charged, condemned 313.

**ensample** *n.* example 421.

**erande** *n.* message 125.

**ermyn** *n.* fur of ermine 412.

**erthe** *n.*[1] earth 371. [OE *eorþ*]

**erthe** *n.*[2] ploughing 373n. [OE *yrþ*]

**es** see *be(n)*

**estres** *n.pl.* paths, recesses of an estate, garden 403. [OF *estre*, 'be', infl. *estrée*, path]

**ete** *inf.* eat 386.

**euen** *n.* vigil, holiday 166; **euenes** *pl.* 310.

**euer** *adv.* always, ever, continually 23, 89, 99.

**F**

**fadir** *n.* father 451; **fadirs** *pl.* 273.

**fayled(e)** *3 sg.pa.* disappointed, failed 102, 155.

**faylynge** *vbl.n.* lack, failure 291.

**fayne** *adj.* glad, eager 402.

**fayntnesse** *n.* cowardice, weakness 21.

**faire** *adj.* attractive, fine, pleasant 272, 429, 434; **faireste** *sup.* 174.

**faire, fayre** *adv.* well, appropriately 226, 462; attractively, pleasingly 66, 82.

**fayth** *n.* allegiance, loyalty 329.

**falles** *3 sg.pr.* falls, comes about 448; **fallyn** *3 pl.pr.* fall 210; **falle** *3 sg.subj.* 198; **felle** *3 pl.pa.* rushed 53; **falles** *3 sg.pr. impers.* befalls 378.

**false** *adj.* deceitful, treacherous 228.

**fare** *n.* feasting, prosperity 295.

**fare** *imper.sg.refl.* go, move 207.

**faste** *adv.* quickly, immediately 217, 367.

**fatt** *adj.* fattened 481.

**fawcons, fawkons** *n.pl.* falcons 92; *gen.pl.* 98.

**fawked** *p.p.* seized by falcons 98.

**feble** *adj.* weak, faint 323.

**feche** *inf.* carry, fetch 449; *3 pl.pr.* acquire 300; **feche forthe** *imper.sg.* bring out, show 281.

**fede** *inf.* feed, support, sustain; *inf. 464*; **feden** *1 pl.pr.* 295; **fede** *3 pl.pr.subj.* 254; **fedde** *p.p.* maintained, patronized 206.

**feghtyn** see **fighte** *inf.*

**fey** *adj.* fated to die 159, 300; mortally wounded 245.

**felawes** *n.pl.* friends, companions 329.

**felde** *n.* battlefield 123, 174; land, farmland 287; **feldes** *pl.* 288; **þe ~ wynn** be victorious 179.

**fele** *adj.* many 35.

**felle** *adj.* wicked, deceitful 228.

**felle** *v.* see **falles**

**ferd** *n.* fear 416.

**ferdede** *p.p.* mustered 138.

**ferdere** *adj.cp.* more intimidated, inspired by fear 287.

**ferdes** *gen.pl.* armies' 123.

**ferdnes** *n.* fear, terror 98.

**fere** *n.*[1] companion, neighbour 311. [OE *geféra*]

**fere** *n.*[2] **in ~** together, in company 21 [OE *gefér*]

**ferlyeste** *adj.sup.* most wonderful, marvellous 102.

**ferre** *adv.* far, afar 416; **ferrere** *cp.* 451.

**ferrere** *adj.cp.* **~ side** other side 311.

**ferse** *adj.* keen, brave 148, 160.

**fesanttes** *n.pl.* pheasants 334.

**festes** *n.pl.* banquets, celebrations 295.

**fewles, fewlis, fewl(l)ys** *n.pl.* wild birds, water birds 44, 91, 96; domestic fowls, chickens 336; **foles** 40n.

**fyfte** *adj.* fifth 174.

**fighte** *n.* battle 148.

**fighte** *inf.* attack, fight 245; **fightis** *3 sg.pr.* 154; **feghtyn** *3 pl.pr.* 160.

**fill** *inf.* satiate, indulge 355; **fille in** *imper.sg.* pour, serve (wine etc.) 281.

**fynde** *inf.* compose 20; come across, find 390, 404, 484; provide for 428; **fynd** *imper.sg.* find 487; **founden** *p.p.* discovered, found 155.

**fyne** *adj.* precious, delicate 92.

**fynger** *n.* finger 480.

**fire** *n.* conflagration, hell-fire 291.

**firste** *adv.* at first, first 291.

**fisches** *n.pl.* fish 386.

**fit(t)** *n.* part of a poem or song 217, 367.

**fyve** *num.* five 206, 329.

**fyvetene** *num.* fifteen 451.

**flakerande** *pr.p.* fluttering, flapping 92. [Cf. OE *flacor, flicorian*]

**fled** *3 sg.pa.* escaped, fled 416.

**flesche** *n.* meat, flesh 336, 346.

**flete** *inf.* swim 386.

**flye** *inf.* **~ forthe** fly away 384.

**flyttynge** *vbl.n.* disputing, arguing 154.

**flode** *n.* river, stream 386.

**florence** *n.pl.* gold coins 281n.

**floures, flowres** *n.pl.* flowers, blossoms 35; ~ **of Fraunse** fleurs-de-lis 78.

**fode** *n.* provisions, food 291, 491.

**folde** *inf.* unfold 35.

**fole** *n.* fool 154.

**foles** see **fewles**

**folke** *n.pl. or coll.* army, men, people, followers 123, 148, 159; nation 138.

**folowe** *inf.* come after, follow 207; obey 395; *2 pl.pr.* take after 273; **folowes** *3 sg.pr.* is loyal 327; **foloen** *3 pl.pr.* 502.

**fongen** *p.p.* caught, trapped 384.

**for** *conj.* because, for, since 5, 56, 107; *prep.* because, because of, on account of, for 44, 55, 98; for the sake of 191, 244, 255; against, in preparation for 275; *with inf.* to, in order to 52, 57, 131.

**forced** *p.p.* reinforced 170.

**forfadirs** *n.pl.* ancestors, forefathers 402.

**forgiffe** *inf.* pardon 135.

**forthe, furthe** *adv.* forward, forth, onward, on 245, 461, 474; further on (in a narrative) 366n; away 384; **forthire** *cp.* further on (in a narrative) 216.

**forthi** *conj.* therefore, accordingly 10, 197, 244; because 286.

**forthir** *inf.* improve, encourage 429, 464.

**foster** *inf.* defend, protect, care for 464; **fosterde** *3 pl.pa.* reared, taught 273; **fosterde** *p.p.* maintained, kept 206.

**fote** *n.* foot 35, **fete** *pl.* 98; **on(e)** ~ walking, on foot 375, 467; **a** ~ **for to holde*** get established, succeed 471.

**foure** *num.* four 77, 329.

**fourme** *n.* retreat, burrow (of a hare) 13.

**fourmed** *p.p.* devised, formed 66.

**fourte** *adj.* fourth 163.

**fre(e)** adj. unrestricted; ~ **londe** freehold land 272; of people, noble in appearance 434.

**freke** *n.* man 287; **frekes** *pl.* soldiers, brave men 102.

**frenchipe** *n.* good will, friendliness 21.

**frende** *n.* comrade, friend 155, 402; **frendes** *pl.* 240.

**freres, freris** *n.pl.* friars 179, 300.

**fresche** *adj.* bright, clear 66; eager, bold 160.

**freschely** *adv.* anew, quickly 217, 367.

**fro** *prep.* away from, from 38, 161; *conj.* because 26, 200.

**frostes** *n.pl.* frosts 275.

**frumentee** *n.* sweetened soup made from grain or milk 334.

**full** *3 sg.pr.subj.* fill, pour (wine etc.) 217n., 367.

**full** *adv.intens. with adj.* very, quite, most 50, 61, 74; *with adv.* very, quite, full 37, 41, 63; **ful** 354, 462.

## G

**gadir** *3 pl.pr.intr.* come together, accumulate 227n.; **gadird** *p.p.* assembled, gathered 432; **gedir** *1 sg.pr.trans.* harvest, gather 231.

**gayly** *adv.* richly, splendidly 62; handsomely 95.

**galegs*** *n.pl.* sandals 157. [OF *galoche*]

**gan** *3 pl.pa.auxil. with inf.* 35.

**gartare** *n.* heraldic representation of the Garter 63, 94; **garters** *pl.* 62.

**gate** *n.* path, street 359.

**gerede** *p.p.adj.* adorned, decorated 63, 94*.

**gete** *inf.* win 173; **getys** *2 sg.pr.* enjoy, earn 440; **getyn** *p.p.* acquired, obtained 269.

**gett** *n.* style, fashion, **of the newe** ~ in the latest style 410.

**giff, gyf** *inf.* give 421, bestow 500; **gyffen** *p.p.* given away, spent 269.

**giftes** *n.pl.* gifts, rewards 500.

**gilt** *n.* offence, crime 135.

**girde** *p.p.* encircled, belted 95.

**girdills** *n.pl.* ornamented belts for the waist or hips 271.

**glade** *adj.* happy, cheerful 440.

**glades** *3 sg.pr.intr.* rejoices 227; **gladdes** *3 sg.pr.trans.* pleases, cheers 391.

**glene** *1 sg.pr.* gather, scrape together 231.

**gleterand** *pr.p.adj.* sparkling, glittering 275.

**God** *n.* God 173, 286, 308.

**god(e), gud(e)** *adj.* fine, excellent *incipit*, prosperous, happy 440; rich, tasty 381, 383; prudent 316; **beste** *sup.* 110, 315, *as n.* þe best 484.

**gold** *adj.* golden, **a** ~ **wyre** gold thread 118n.

**golde** *n.* gold 61, 86, 271; (her.) the tincture *or* 75; gold thread, fine wire 63, 92.

**gome** *n.* warrior, soldier 118; man 359, 391.

**goo** *inf.* pass, go 231, 406; **go** *imper.sg.* 105.

**goullyng** *vbl.n.* blaring of trumpets 359. [ON *gaula*]

grace *n.* favour, mercy 135, 371, 399; ~ **appon grounde** victory 173.

gray *adj.* dull, grey 381.

graunte *inf.* permit, grant 371, 399; **grounden** *p.p.* promised, granted 269.

grene *adj.* green 48; *as n.* 149.

grete *adj.* magnificent 94, 500; powerful, imposing 95; fast, rapid 122; *as adv.* much, greatly 224.

greues *3 sg.pr.* injures, annoys 391.

grewell *n.* thin porridge 381.

grounde *n.* battlefield 173; earth, ground 411.

grounden see **graunte**

grow(e) *inf.* grow 371, 399; **growes** *3 sg.pr.* 397.

gude *n.* property, money 271; **gudes, gudis** *pl.* possessions, profit, produce 227, 265, 441. See also **god** *adj.*

## ʒ

ʒalowe *adj.* yellow 75.

ʒape *adj.* clever, ingenious 75; **ʒapeste** *sup.* most astute 119.

ʒarked *p.p.adj.* made, adorned 75.

ʒe *pron. 2 pl.nom.* you 134, 198, 218; **ʒow** *acc.* 31, 135, 197; **ʒowe** *dat.* 228, 284; **ʒour(e)** *gen.* 129, 219, 273.

ʒee *adv.* yes 246, 294, 368.

ʒeme *inf.* protect, guard, care for 114, 152, 419; **ʒemes** *3 pl.pr.* 376.

ʒerdes *n.pl.* yards, enclosures 289.

ʒere *n.* year, season 374; **ʒeris** *gen.sg.* 387; *pl.* 119, 369.

ʒis *adv.* yes 108.

ʒit(t) *adv.* yet 174, 454.

ʒondere *adj.* yonder 105; *adv.* 143.

ʒonge *adj.* young 398; **ʒongeste** *sup.* 119.

ʒore *adv.* a long time ago 321, 445.

ʒour(e), ʒow see **ʒe**

## H

haf(e), haue *inf.* have, possess, behave 256, 279, 348; **hafe** *1 sg.pr.* 136; **haste** *2 sg.pr.* 248, 261, 290; **has(e)** *3 sg.* 145, 155, 158, **hath(e)** 297, 323; **hafe** *2 pl.* 361; *3 pl.* 271, 425, **hathe** 3n.; **haue** *2 sg.subj.* 269; **haue, have** *3 sg.subj.pr.* 68, 485; **had** *3 sg.pa.* 58, 116, 404; **haden** *2 pl.* 272, **had** *3 pl.pa.* 409.

halfe *adj.* half 387.

halpeny *n.* halfpenny 387.

hande, honde *n.* hand 87, 121, 419;

handes *pl.* 211, 268; **harde appone** ~ very soon 11.

handil *inf.* manipulate 413.

happede *p.p.* covered up 298.

happyns *3 sg.pr.impers.* befalls 471.

harde *adj.* difficult 374, 413; ~ **hattes** helmets 51.

harde *adv.* close 11; soundly 435; very 454.

hare *n.* hare 404; **hares** *pl.* 13.

harme *n.* calumny, slander 68.

harmes *3 sg.pr.impers.* injures, grieves 454.

hasteleteʒ *n.pl.* pieces of meat (? entrails of a boar) roasted on a spit 492. [OF *hastelet*]

hate *1 sg.pr.* detest, hate 455.

hates *n.pl.* feelings of hatred, enmity 219.

hathe see **hafe**

hathell *n.* man 68, warrior 70.

hatt *1 sg.pr.* am called 222; **hatten** *2 pl.* 218.

hatte *n.* hat, (her.) chapeau, cap of maintenance 72, 73; **hattes** *pl.* helmets 51.

hattfull *adj.* wrathful 73.

hauande *vbl.n.* possessions 323.

haule *n.* hall 364.

hawberkes *n.pl.* coats of mail 50.

hawthorne *n.* hawthorn tree 36.

he *pron. 3 sg.masc.nom.* he 9, 26, 27; **hym** *acc., dat.* 88, 101, 102; *refl.* 109, 241; **his, hys** *gen.* 8, 72, 89; **hymseluen** *pron.* himself 28, 173.

hede *n.* head 36, 72, 332, leader 147; **hedes** *pl.* 51, 150, 175. See also **bede-hede, tonne-hede.**

hedir(e) *adv.* here, hither 162, 197.

hee see **wee hee**

heghe, hye *adj.* tall, great 237; arrogant 246; exorbitant 372; *adv.* high 42, 372, loudly 358; **vpon** ~ high up 70, **one** ~ loudly 40.

heghwalles *n.pl.* woodpeckers 38.

held see **holden**

helys *n.pl.* heels 450.

helle *n.* hell 260, 261, 444.

helme *n.* helmet 72, 76, **helmys** *pl.* 51.

helpe *n.* aid, benefit 361.

helpe *inf.* assist, support 169, avail 154; **helpis** *3 sg.pr.* 222.

heltre *n.* halter 418.

hem see **thay**

hend *adj. as sb.* noble, gracious one 419.

hen(n)(e) *n.* domestic hen, chicken 347, 387, 482.

**henppe** *n.* hemp, fibre 145.
**henttis** *3 sg.pr.* takes hold of 211; **hent** *3 sg.subj.* embrace 447.
**herdmans** *n.gen.sg.* of a retainer, a member of a household 364. [OE *hīred-man*]
**here** *n.* army 50, 58, 196.
**here** *inf.* hear 8, 20, 220; **heris** *2 sg.pr.* 319; **herd** *1 sg.pa.* 364; **herde** *3 sg.* 23.
**here** *adv.* here, in this place *incipit*, 130, 138; at this time 18, in this world 260, 298, 444.
**herede** see **white-herede**
**heres** *n.pl.* men, noblemen; in direct address, sirs 212.
**herouns** *n.pl.* herons 492.
**hert(e)** *n.* heart, spirit, courage 21, 88, 227; **hertis** *pl.* 19, 219, 406.
**herthe-stones** *n.pl.* hearth-stones 13.
**herueste** *n.* harvest, crop 274.
**heselis** *n.pl.* hazel bushes 38.
**hete** *2 sg.pr.* order 279n.; **hetys** *3 sg.* 211. [OE *hātan*, pa. *hēt*]
**hethe** *n.* field, battlefield 58*, 196.
**hethyng** *n.* contempt, scorn 68.
**heu*** *n.* colour 64n. [OE *hīw*]
**heuen** *n.* heaven 244, 255, 415; *gen.sg.* 361.
**hewen** *p.p.* cut, struck 196.
**hidde** *p.p.* concealed 298.
**hyeghte** *3 sg.pr.* approaches, comes quickly 11; **hyes** passes 453; **hy** *2 sg.pr.subj.refl.* hurry 467.
**hye** see **heghe**
**hightilde** *p.p.* prepared, fitted out 438.
**hill** *n.* mound covered with plants 36n. [? OE *\*hygel*]
**hillede** *3 sg.pa.* covered, protected 76.
**hym, hym, hymseluen** see **he**
**hyne** *n.* household 438; *pl.* members of a household, servants 212. [OE *hīwan*]
**hipped** *3 pl.pa.* leapt, hopped 38.
**hir** see **sche**
**hir(e)** see **thay**
**hyrne** *n.* corner 238.
**his, hys** see **he**
**hodirde** *p.p.* covered, heaped up 298.
**holde(n)** *inf.* remain 9n.; **hold(e)** *1 sg.pr.* consider 154, 446; **held** *3 sg.pa.* held, guided 419; **hold** *3 sg.pr.subj.* possess, enjoy 447; **holde ... fot** (fig.) keep pace 471*n.
**holy** *adj.* ~ **kirke** the church of Rome 147.
**holt(e)** *n.* wood, grove 50, 404; wooded hill 70. [OE *holt*; cf. ON *holt*]

**home** *n.* home 236, native country 161, 467.
**honde** see **hande**
**honge** *inf.* hang, kill 374; **hengeth** *3 sg.pr.* hangs, is suspended 184, **hynges** 251; **hanged** *p.p.* 260, **hynged** 145.
**hope** *inf.* expect, want 374; *1 sg.pr.* believe 11, 147, 413; ~ **aftir** *imper.sg.* expect 290.
**hore** *adj.* grey with age 9.
**horse** *n.* horse 467.
**hot(t)e** *adj.* hot 351, 444; violent 219.
**houes** *3 sg.pr.* lingers, waits 105, 123, 143.
**house, howse** *n.* household 212, 347; **houses, howses** *pl.* buildings 250, 438, as property to be let 237.
**how** *adv.* in what manner 416; at what price 233.
**howes** *n.pl.* lawyers' coifs 150.
**howndes** *n.pl.* dogs 237.
**hungere** *n.* hunger, shortage of food 237.
**hungry** *adj. as n.* those who are hungry 482.
**hurcle** *inf.* nestle, crouch 13. [unkn.; cf. Du., MLG *hurken*]
**hurdes** *n.pl.* buttocks 436. [Cf. Sc. *hurdeis, hurdies*]

### I

**I** *pron. 1 sg.nom.* 11, 31, 32; **me** *acc.* and *dat.* 31, 47, 93; **my** *gen.* 35, 104, 108; **myn** (before vowels and **h**) 36, 45, 137; **myn one** on my own 32.
**iche** *adj.* each, every 278, 287, 404, ~ **a** 63, 81, 249; *pron.* each (one) 145, 158.
**icheon, ichone** *pron.* each one 6, 62, 93.
**if** *conj.* if 100, 107, 131.
**ylike** *adv.* evenly, equally 48.
**ymbryne** *adj.* ~ **dayes** ember days, days of fasting 310.
**in** *prep.* in 3, 13, 15; into 46, 53, 77; by 140, at 373.
**ynche** *n.* inch 341.
**inde, ynde** *n.* indigo, indigo-coloured fabric 62, 94.
**ynewe** *adj.* sufficient, many 84, 282, 405.
**into** *prep.* into 261, 474.
**inwith** *adv.* within 117.
**iren, yren** *n.* iron, blade 185, armour 111.
**it** *pron. 3 sg.neut.* 1, 16, 18; *impers.* 11, 178, 308.
**itwiste*** *adv.* amongst, together with 317.

## J

**jay(e)** *n.* jay 26, 40.
**jangle** *inf.* chatter 26; **janglede** *3 sg.pa.* 40.
**japes** *n.pl.* light entertainment, jokes 26.
**jarmede** *3 pl.pa.* chirped, twittered 40n. [unkn. cf. ON *járma*, OF *gemir*]
**joynede** *p.p.adj.* fastened 115.
**jupown** *n.* tunic 115.
**juste** *adj.* close-fitting 115.

## K

**kayre(n)** see **cayre**
**kaysser** *n.* emperor 327.
**katour** *n.* purveyor, caterer 491.
**kembid** *p.p.adj.* combed 151.
**ken** *3 pl.pr.* know, recognize 462; *imper.sg.* introduce 479, direct 491.
**kene** *adj.* fierce, savage 74, 237; intense 275.
**kepe** *inf.* maintain, accommodate 462; *3 sg.subj.* protect, preserve 69, 124.
**kerpede** see **carpe**
**kydde** *p.p.adj.* recognized 315.
**kiddes** *n.pl.* young goats 340.
**kynde** *adj.* natural 274; **in the ~** (her.) in a natural fashion 117n.
**kyng(e)** *n.* king 69, 86, 90; **kynges** *pl.* 503, *gen.pl.* 3.
**kyngdome** *n.* realm, kingdom 132.
**kirke** *n.* cathedral 503; **holy ~** 147.
**kyrtill** *n.* tunic 90n.
**kystes** *n.pl.* coffers, chests 255.
**kyth(e)** *n.* country, homeland 69, 124, 134.
**kythe** *inf.* make known, proclaim 104; *imper.pl.* 218.
**knafe** *n.* servant, attendant 485.
**knawen** *inf.* know, understand, recognize 491; **knowe** *1 sg.pr.* 468, *1 pl.pr.* 205, *2 pl.pr.* 134; **knowes** *3 pl.pr.* 490; **knewe** *1 sg.pa.* 83, 118, 187; **knawen(n), knowen** *p.p.* 29, 315, 326.
**knees** *n.pl.* knees 210.
**knyghte** *n.* knight 83*, 103, 327; **knyghtis, knyghtes** *pl.* 203, 502.
**knoke** *n.* blow, a beating 485.
**knoppe** *n.* knob, stud 81.

## L

**lache** *inf.* catch 406; **laughte** *3 sg.pa.* took up, accepted 286.
**ladde** *n.* servant 388; **laddes** *pl.* men of low birth 375, 378.

**lady** *n.* **oure ~** the Virgin Mary 177, 415; **ladyes** *pl.* women of high birth 15, 409.
**laye** *inf.* lay, place 284; **layde** *1 sg.pa.* 36.
**laye** see also **lygge**
**lande, lond(e)** *n.* country, nation 15, 19, 152; land, property 133, 272, 284; **londes** *pl.* farmlands 234.
**lanterne** *n.* lamp 306.
**laped** *3 sg.pa.* enclosed 111; **lapped** *p.p.* 350.
**larkes** *n.pl.* skylarks 350.
**last(e)** *adj. as n.* **at the ~** finally, in the end 29, 45, 399.
**lasteth** *3 sg.pr.* endures 7.
**late, let** *imper.sg.* allow, let 256, 320, 378, make 486; **~ be** cease from 255, 263; **~ goo** *inf.* release 406; **lattys goo** *3 sg.pr.* 231; **lett of** *p.p.* regarded 27.
**late** *adv.* late 306.
**lattere** *adj.cp. as sb.* newcomer 29.
**la(u)nde** *n.* glade, clearing 48, 54, 209; open area in forest 405.
**lawe** *n.* hill, earthworks 49n. [OE *hlǣw, hlǣw*]
**lawe** *adj.* low 111.
**lawes** *n.pl.* laws 152.
**lebarde** *n.* leopard, (her.) lion 74; **leberdes** *pl.* 80.
**lede** *n.*[1] seal 146.
**lede** *n.*[2] man 108, 428, 459; in direct address, man, sir 369, 466; **ledis** *pl.* 88, 152, 177*, **ledys** 29.
**lede** *inf.* guide, lead 128, 497, marry 15; **ledis** *2 sg.pr.* 270; *3 sg.* 148; **ledith** *3 sg.pr.* 171.
**ledyng** *vbl.n.* guidance 223.
**leefe** *adj.* eager, ready 465.
**lefe** *n.* **~ take** leave 469.
**legges** *n.pl.* limbs 111.
**legyance** *n.* allegiance 501.
**ley** *adj.* fallow 234.
**lelely** *adv.* faithfully 430.
**lemman** *n.* mistress, sweetheart 428.
**lenede** *p.p.* given permission or listened to 27n.
**lenge** *inf.* stay, dwell 469.
**lenger, lengeste** see **longe**
**lengthe** *n.* distance 49, 54.
**lere** *inf.* teach, guide 223.
**lesse** *adv.* lest 98, 395.
**lethire** *n.* leather 184.
**let(t)** see **late**
**lettres** *n.pl.* letters of the alphabet 66; messages 466.

**leue** *v.*[1] *imper.sg.* believe 259.

**leue** *v.*[2] *inf.* forsake 422; **leued(e)** *3 sg.pa.* left aside 209, 286.

**lyes** see **lygge**

**life, lyfe, lyue** *n.* life 108, 133, 385.

**lyfe, lyve** *inf.* behave, live 225, 375, 378; **lyfe** *2 sg.subj.* 259; **life** *3 sg.subj.* 243.

**lygge** *inf.* lie, remain, rest 463; **liggen, ligges** *3 pl.* 234, 503; **laye** *1 sg.pa.* 45; *3 sg.* was situated 49; **lyes** *3 sg.pr.impers.* is fitting 428.

**lighte** *adj.* nimble, sprightly 74.

**lighte** *p.p.adj.* lighted 306.

**lightten** *inf.* cheer 406; **lighten doun** *3 pl.pr.* dismount 209.

**lykes** *3 sg.pr.* likes 495; *impers.* pleases 279, 352, **lyketh** 125.

**lympe** *inf.* become 369; **lympis, lympes** *3 sg.impers.* befalls 284, 449.

**lyngwhittes** *n.pl.* linnets 350. [from OE *hlinc* + *hwīt*]

**lyre** *n.* misfortune 415n.

**liste** *3 sg.pr.impers.subj.* please 378.

**lite*** *adj.* few 369.

**littill-whattes** *phr.* trifles, small amounts 225n.

**lofte** *n.* in **one** ~, **appon** ~ up high, on top 72, 80, 150.

**loken** see **lowked**

**lokes, lukes** *3 sg.pr.* looks, gazes 324, 415, 456; **loke, luke** *imper.sg.* ensure, take heed 466, 475, 485; **lokande** *pr.p.* glaring 74.

**lokkes** *n.pl.* hairs, tufts of fur 71.

**lomes** *n.pl.* tools, looms 234.

**lond(e)** see **lande**

**longe** *adj.* long, elongated 74; *adv.* for a long time 243; **lenger, lengare** *cp.* 259, 488; **lengest** *sup.* 449.

**loo** *exclam.* lo! 124, 326.

**lorde** *n.* lord, leader 69, 95, 108; **oure** ~ God 124, 285; **lordes, lordis** *pl.* 19, 54, 223.

**losse** *inf.* lose 133.

**loue** *n.* love 244.

**loue** *inf.* love, cherish 430; **lufe** *1 sg.pr.* 225, **loueste** *2 sg.pr.* 328; **loueth** *3 sg.* 88; **louen, lufen** *3 pl.* 177, 501; **louediste** *2 sg.pa.* 304; **louede** *3 sg.pa.* 286; **loued** *3 pl.pa.* 19; **loued(e)** *p.p.* 459, esteemed 27.

**loueliche** *adj.* pleasant 48; **louelyeste** *sup.* most attractive 88; **louely** *adv.* affectionately 456.

**lowe** *adv.* **on(e)** ~ below 80, 184.

**lowked** *3 pl.pa.* closed 45; **loken** *p.p.* enclosed 49.

**lukes** see **lokes**

## M

**machen** *inf.* match, ~ **agayne** pit against 172.

**madde** *adj.* foolish 446.

**may** *auxil.vb.* *2 sg.pr.* can, may 484; *3 sg.* 154, 243, 299; **myghte** *1 sg.pa.* 43.

**mayne*** *n.* strength 166n.

**make** *n.* mistress 446.

**make** *inf.* cause, make 373, 431, 463; **madiste** *2 sg.pa.* brought about 264; **made** *3 sg.pa.* composed, wrote 28; **maken dele** *3 pl.pr.* offer donations 303.

**makers** *n.pl.* composers, writers 20.

**man** *n.* man, person 28, warrior 172; **men** *pl.* 193, 233, 242; **mens** *gen.pl.* 337.

**many** *adj.* many 4, 141, 153; ~ **a** (with sg.) 168.

**mantill** *n.* sleeveless robe 90.

**marchandes** *n.pl.* merchants 377; **merchandes** *gen.pl.* 190.

**mare** see **more**

**mater** *n.* affair, matter 264; **matirs** *pl.* stories, narratives 20.

**mawes** *n.pl.* stomachs 355.

**mawmene*** *n.* dish of diced meat and wine and/or almond milk 355.

**mawngery** *n.* feast 304.

**medewe** *n.* meadow 34.

**meles** *n.pl.* meals 365.

**melleste** *2 sg.pr.* speak, complain 264.

**mend** *inf.* improve 383.

**mery** *adj.* riotous 365.

**merke** *n.* mark = 160 pence 356.

**merkes*** *n.pl.* insignia, emblems 190.

**meruelle** *n.* a wonderful thing 344.

**mese** *n.* course 344, 356.

**mete** *n.* meat, flesh 335, 345, 383.

**mete** *inf.* engage in battle, attack 52.

**myddes, myddis** *n.* centre 164, **in the** ~ at the waist 95.

**myghte** see **may**

**myle** *n.* mile 49, 451.

**myndale** *n.* commemorative feast 304n.

**myrthe** *n.* pleasure, amusement 304; **myrthes** *n.pl.* literary diversions 20.

**myster** *n.* need 361.

**molde** *n.* earth 172.

**monethe** *n.* month 276.

**more** *adj.cp.* greater 293, 407; more 271, 323, 417; *as sb.* 489; **moste** *sup.* most 166, 473; **more, mare** *adv.cp.* more 28, 305, 323; **moste** *sup.* 459.

**morow** *n.* morning 478.

**morsell** *n.* tasty piece 383.

**moste** *1 sg.pr.* must 345; *3 sg.* 283, 390*n.

**mournes** *3 sg.pr.* is worried, anxious about 446.

**N**

**nade** *2 sg.pa.* had not 438.

**nappe** *inf.* sleep 43; **nappen** *2 pl.pr.* 435.

**ne** *adv.* not 9, 47, 107; *conj.* nor 8, 23, 127*n.

**nedles** *adj.* excessive 338.

**nedeles** *adv.* in vain 401.

**negardes** *n.pl.* misers 435. [cf. Sw. *njug*, ON *hnöggr* 'stingy', Sw. dial. *niggla* 'be stingy']

**neghe** *inf.* approach 18; ~ **nerre** *3 pl.pr.subj.* close for battle 106; **neghande** *pr.ptc.* 43.

**neghe** *adv.* soon 16; nearly 18.

**nekke** *n.* neck, **in the** ~ over the neck 76, close into the neck 151.

**nerre** *adv.cp.* closer 106, 127.

**neuer** *adv.* never 4, 7, 22, not at all 106.

**new** *adj.* new, new-fangled 410.

**newely** *adv.* soon 18.

**nyghte, nyȝte** *n.* evening, night 43, 248, 306; **nyghttis** *pl.* 266.

**nyne** *adj.* ninth 4.

**nysely** *adv.* extravagantly 410.

**nysottes** *n.pl.* fools 410.

**no** *adj.* no, none 7, 11, 21; *adv.* no more 305, 452; **none** *adv.* ~ **nerre** any closer 127.

**noghte, not(t)** *adv.* not 134, 224, 273; **noghte** *pron.* nothing 346.

**note** *n.* business, affair 338.

**noþer, nothire** *adj.* **in no** ~ nothing else 11, 178, 239.

**now(e)** *adv.* now, at this time 4, 5, 21; **now** *interj.* 69, 221.

**no(w)thir** *adj.* neither 201, 327.

**O**

**of** *prep.* of 2, 10, 14; made of 62, 64, 81; through 135, 371; about, concerning 264; on account of 426; from 138, 139, 140; **off** from 202; **out** ~ away from 416, 484, 489; **off** *adv.* away, off 183.

**ofte** *adv.* repeatedly, frequently 241, 422.

**ogh** *3 sg.pr.* ought 287; **owethe** owns 199, 347; **owthe** *3 pl.pr.* owe 329; **aughte** *3 sg.pa.* conquered 1.

**oke** *n.* oak tree(s) 397.

**one** *adj.* one, a single 67, 107, 127, alone 132, 135, own 32; *pron.* 88, 102, 145.

**on(e)** *prep.* on 36, 39, 48, in 110, at 122, to 445; ~ **heghe** 40, 73; ~ **lowe** 80, 184; ~ **lofte** 80, 150.

**ones** *adv.* once 31, 127, 299, 364*.

**opynes** *3 sg.pr.* opens 232.

**or** *conj.*[1] or 18, 280, 284.

**or** *conj.*[2] before 43, 84, 229.

**ordire** *n.* religious order 186.

**orfraied*** *adj.* embroidered with gold 79n. [from OF *orfrois*]

**oþer, owthere, owthir** *conj.* or 290, 300, 482.

**other(e), oþer** *adj.* other, another 179, 188, 193; *pron.* 6, 58, 286, **othire** 38.

**ouer** *prep.* over, across 460.

**ouerbrade** *p.p.adj.* covered, laden 342.

**oughte** *pron.* anything 186.

**oure** see **we**

**ourlede** *p.p.adj.* trimmed, lined 412.

**out, owt(e)** *adv.* out 52, 82, 416; *prep.* ~ **of** from 79, 484.

**ownn** *adj.* own 400; **myn one** alone 32.

**owthe** see **ogh**

**owthir(e)** *adj.* each 196; *pron.* either 245. Cf. also **ayther(e)**.

**owttrage** *n.* excess, prodigality 267.

**P**

**paye** *inf.* please, gratify 408, pay 486; **payes** *3 sg.pr.impers.* pleases 297, 433; **payen** *1 pl.pr.* 427; **payede fore** *p.p.* 283.

**payntten** *inf.* decorate, paint 301; **paynted** *p.p.* 65.

**pales** *n.* palace 498.

**paradyse** *n.* heaven 296.

**pared** *p.p.* trimmed 183.

**parischen** *n.* parishioner 376.

**parte** *n.* share 256, 297, 382.

**passe** *3 sg.pr.subj.* pass, go 372, 476, 486; *imper.sg.* 461, 490.

**pawnce** *n.* armour covering abdomen 112.

**pedders** *n.pl.* pedlars 377.

**pelers** *n.pl.* pillars, columns 301.

**peloure** *n.* fur 393.

**pendant** *n.* end of a belt 183n.

**peny** *n.* penny 487.

**penyles** *adj.* destitute 393.

**peple** *n.* people 256, 297, 370; retainers, supporters 433.

**pergett** *inf.* plaster 301.

**perle** *n.* pearl 81.

**pertly** *adv.* boldly, audaciously 129.

**pertrikes** *n.pl.* partridges 493.

**pese** *n.* truce 55; civil peace 129, 318.

**petit*** *adj.* insignificant 476.

**pik** *imper.sg.* rob 486.

**pysayne** *n.* armour covering neck and breast 112.

**plates** *n.pl.* plates of armour 114.

**plenté** *n.* abundance 370.

**plesynge** *pr.p.adj.* gratifying 296.

**plontes** *n.pl.* vegetables 332.

**plouers** *n.pl.* plovers 493.

**plunket** *n.* lead grey or light blue 65.

**poyntes** *n.pl.* dots 65; pointed ends, tips 183.

**poles** *inf.* pools, reservoirs 235.

**polischede** *p.p.adj.* polished 112.

**pompe** *n.* display, vainglory 422.

**pope** *n.* Pope 169, 461.

**po(u)re** *adj.*[1] insufficient, thin 420; destitute 393; *as sb.* 256, 258, 295.

**poure** *adj.*[2] complete, perfect 370. [OF *pur*]

**pouert(e)** *n.* poverty 382, 422.

**powere** *n.* army 318; **powers** *pl.* 129.

**prayed** *3 pl.pa.* prayed, hoped 55.

**prechours** *n.pl.* preachers 169.

**prelates** *n.pl.* bishops 376.

**prestes** *n.pl.* priests 376.

**pride, pryde** *n.* ostentation, display 14, 230, 267.

**pryke** *1 sg.pr.* tie up, fasten 232n.; **prik-kede** *1 sg.pa.* spurred, rode out 318.

**prynce** *n.* ruler, lord 55; Christ 296.

**pryne** *1 sg.pr.* sew up 232n.

**pris** *n.* price, cost 372; *of* ~ wealthy 377.

**priste** *adj.* inclined, willing 169. [OF *prest*]

**pro(u)de, prowde** *adj.* rich, of high degree 377; elegant, magnificent 433; great 498.

**pulled** *p.p.adj.* plucked 493.

**pultrie** *n.* place where fowls are sold; street of this name in Cheapside 490.

**purse** *n.* money-bag 162, 232, 487.

**put** *imper.sg.* ~ **owte his eghe** deceive 487.

**Q**

**quarterd** *p.p.adj.* quartered 340.

**quarters** *n.pl.* quarters of an escutcheon 77.

**quod** *3 sg.pa.* said 246, 263, 294.

**R**

**rayled(e)** *p.p.adj.* decorated, adorned 60, 343.

**rayse** *v.* raise, lift; **raysen** *2 pl.pr.* 436; *imper.sg.* restore, establish 289; **raysed** *p.p.* organized 438.

**rane** *3 sg.pa.* flowed 41.

**ranke** *adj.* abundant 322.

**rathere** *adv.cp.* sooner 322.

**ratouns** *n.pl.* rats 254.

**raughten** see **rechen**

**rawnsom** *n.* a large sum 363.

**raxillyng** *vbl.n.* stretching 436.

**rechen** *2 pl.pr.* give, pay 363; **raughten** *3 pl.pa.* reached, rose up 42.

**rede** *n.* red 60; *adj.* fine 380.

**rede** *inf.* advise, rule 57; **redde** *p.p.* read, found 23.

**redy** *adj.* ready, eager 278.

**refreyte** *n.* theme, treatment of a theme *incipit.*

**reghte** *adv.* just, precisely 165.

**rekken** *inf.* describe, account for 192, 344.

**reme** *inf.* weep, lament 258.

**renke** *n.* man, warrior 23, 100, 202; **renkes** *pl.* 270.

**renthowses** *n.pl.* houses for lease 289.

**repaste** *n.* feast 363.

**rere** *imper.sg.* set up, establish 474; **rerede** *p.p.* 59.

**reuere** *n.* riverbank (place for hawking) 100.

**rewlyn** *inf.* control 57.

**rewme** *n.* kingdom 128.

**rewthe** *n.* pity 258.

**ryall(e)** *adj.* sumptuous, rare 339; *adv.* proudly, arrogantly 128.

**riche** *adj.* proud, rich, powerful 132, 191, 263, **ryche** 134; rich (of food), tasty 334, 339; sumptuous 348, 394; **richere** *adj.cp.* 322; **riche** *adv.* richly 63, 94*.

**rychely*** *adv.* splendidly 270.

**ridde** *inf.* part combatants 57. [ON *ryðja*]

**ryde** *inf.* ride (with an armed band) 131; **ryden** *3 pl.pr.* 360; **ryde** *3 sg.subj.pr.* 100.

**rye** *n.* rye 380.

**ryfe** *n.* quantity 258.
**rigge** *n.* back 340.
**ryme** *imper.sg.* ~ **vp** clear out 289.
**rynges** *n.pl.* rings 343.
**ryse** *inf.* rise up, stand 211.
**ristyth** *3 sg.pr.* lies, is found; **where þe wronge** ~, on which side the fault lies 200.
**rode** *n.* cross 343.
**rofe** *n.* roof 60, 251.
**romance** *n.* romance, poem 23.
**roste** *n.* roast meat 339.
**rote** *3 sg.subj.* rot 254.
**roughe** *n.* husk 380; *adj.* turbulent 42.
**rownde** *adv.* smoothly, evenly 183.
**roungen** *3 pl.pr.* gnaw 39n.
**routten** *2 pl.pr.* snore 436.
**rowte** *n.* troop, band, company 128, 202, 270.
**ruyde** *adj.* violent, rough 42.
**ruste** *3 sg.subj.* rust 254.

## S

**sable** *n.* black, (her.) sable 157.
**sad(d)e** *adj.* heavy 146; resolute 193; **sadly** *adv.* earnestly, seriously 17; deeply 215.
**sadills** *n.pl.* saddles 394.
**safe, saue** *prep.* except 238, 347, 418.
**say** *inf.* tell, speak, declare 178, 360; *1 sg.pr.* 146; **says(e)** *3 sg.* 325, 457; **sayne** *2 pl.pr.* 399; **sayen** *3 pl.pr.* 159; **say** *3 sg.subj.* 18; **said(e), sayd(e)** *1 sg.pa.* 99, *3 sg.* 108, 124, 212; **sayden** *3 pl.pa.* 204; **sayde** *p.p.* 10, 321.
**sayntes** *n.pl.* saints 310.
**sakkes** *n.pl.* sacks 250.
**samen** *adv.* together 360.
**sandisman** *n.* messenger 204.
**saue** *2 pl.pr.* preserve, save 401; **saued** *2 pa.* 444.
**sawe** *n.* proverb, saying 10; motto 67.
**schadewe*** *inf.* shelter, provide shade for 400.
**schake** *inf.* go, ride 403.
**schalkes** *n.pl.* men 317, 432.
**schal(l)** *1 sg.pr.* shall, will 31, 220, 247; **schall** *2 sg.* 260, 426; **schalte** 279; **sall** *3 sg.* 369, **schal(l)** 9, 27, 130; **schall** *1 pl.pr.* 207, 458, *2 pl.* 458; **s(c)hal(l)** *3 pl.* 12, 13, 179; **scholde*** *2 sg.pr.subj.* 472; **scholde** *1 sg.pa.* 178, *2 sg.* 257, **scholdeste** 258; **schold** *3 sg.* 388, *3 pl.* 152, 384; **scholde** *3 sg.pa.subj.* 253.

**schame** *n.* disgrace 400, 432.
**scharpynynge** *vbl.n.* sharpening 185.
**schathed** *p.p.* disgraced 362.
**schauynge** *pr.p.adj.* ~ **iren** razor 185.
**schawe** *n.* wood, thicket 403; **schawes** *pl.* 53.
**schenchipe** *n.* ignominy, disgrace 432.
**schent** *p.p.* disgraced, punished 317.
**schetys** *n.p.* sheets 463.
**schewe** *v.* show, point out, teach, demonstrate; **schewe** *inf.* 281, 403, 421; **schewes** *2 sg.pr.* 422; **schew** *imper.sg.* 481.
**schiltrons** *n.pl.* phalanxes, troops in close array 53.
**schynethe** *3 sg.pr.* gleams 185.
**scho** *pron. 3 sg.fem.nom.* she 416, 420, 430; **hir** *acc.* her 447; **hir** *gen.* 415, 416, 418.
**scholdirs** *n.pl.* forelegs 481.
**schonn** *inf.* avoid 432.
**schorte** *adj.* brief *incipit.*
**schowen** *3 pl.pr.* push, march forward 53.
**scorned** *3 pl.pr.* mocked, scorned 362.
**sectours, sektours** *n.pl.* executors 302, 443.
**see** *n.* ocean 312.
**see** *inf.* see, observe, look 8, 17, 299, 434*; *1 sg.pr.* 157, 337, **se** 321; **sawe** *1 sg.pa.* 137, **seghe** 188, **see** 83; **sawe** *3 sg.* 89; **sene** *p.p.* 3.
**seere** *adj.* various 3.
**sege** *n.* seat 483.
**segge** *n.* man 89, 192, 337; in direct address, sir 137.
**sekere** *adj.* resolute 193.
**selcouthes** *n.pl.* marvels 3.
**seldom** *adv.* rarely 160.
**sele** *n.* prosperity 204.
**seled** *p.p.adj.* fastened, sealed 146.
**sell(e)** *inf.* sell 284, 401; **sellyn** *2 pl.pr.* 396; **sellen** *3 pl.* 233; **solde** *p.p.* 234, 261, 407.
**selly** *adj.* marvellous 99.
**semys** *3 sg.pr.* seems, appears 178; **semede** *3 pl.pa.* 97, **semyde** *with pron.sb. in acc.* 176.
**sen** *conj.* since 134.
**send** *inf.* send 8; **sende** *1 sg.pr.* 466; **sendes*** *3 sg.* 125n; **send** *imper.sg.* 483.
**sendale, sendell** *n.* silken material 180, 394.
**septure** *n.* sceptre 87.
**sercles** *n.pl.* rings 394.
**serue** *inf.* serve 177, 388; prepare 492.

**sett** *v.* seat, place, settle; **sett** *imper.sg.* 483; **sett** *p.p.* 87, 188, 335, leased 407.

**seuen** *adj.* seven 299.

**seuer** *inf.refl.* scatter, disperse 443.

**sewes** *n.pl.* soups, broths 339, 381.

**sexe** *adj.* six 157, 337; **sexte** sixth 180.

**siche** *adj.* such 137, 165, 251; *as sb.* such a thing 421.

**syde** *n.* side 193, 311; **sydes** *pl.* 60, sides of the body 115; þi ~ your body 463.

**syde*** *adj.* ample, long 411.

**syghte** *n.* spectacle 137; vision 455.

**siluer(e)** *n.* silver 214, 363, 500*, money 256, 427.

**silk(e)** *n.* silk 82, 414; **silken** *adj.* 463, covered in silk 87.

**symple** *adj.* humble 414.

**synes** *n.pl.* symbols, insignia 188.

**synn** *n.* sin 261, 313.

**sir** *n.* (title) sir 204, 452.

**sythen** *conj.* since 1, 169, 427; *adv.* then, afterwards 276, 479, 483.

**skathill** *adj.* wicked 443.

**skyll** *n.* reason, discrimination 362.

**slabbande** *adj.* trailing 411.

**slee** *adj.* subtle, misleading 6.

**slees** *3 sg.pr.* destroys 302.

**sleght** *p.p.adj.* let down 411.

**sleues** *n.pl.* sleeves 411.

**smytte** *inf.* strike, fight 431.

**snyppes** *n.pl.* snipes 349. [unkn. cf. ON *mýrisnípa*]

**so** *adv.* so, to such an extent 4, 42, 126; so, like this 180.

**softe** *adv.* comfortably, gently 483.

**sogoure** *n.* syrup 350.

**soyle** *n.* earth 401.

**some** *pron.* some 189, 190, 254.

**someris** *n.gen.sg.* summer's 165.

**sone** *n.* son 8, 302; **sones** *pl.* 400.

**sone** *adv.* at once 85, 231.

**sonn(e)** *n.* sun 33, 89, 165.

**sore** *adj.* miserable 454.

**sorowe** *n.* sorrow, misery 331, 407.

**sothe** *n.* truth 17, 178, 181; *adj.* true 321; **sothe*** *adv.* surely 357.

**soule** *n.* soul, spirit 261, 455.

**sowrede** *3 sg.pa.* stung, bleared 215n.

**sowes** *3 sg.pr. with coll.sb.* plant 370.

**sowme** *n.* total 192.

**sowpped** *1 sg.pa.* drank 215.

**southewarde** *adv.* southward 8.

**spare** *inf.intr.* save 224; *trans.* **spareste** *2 sg.pr.* 260; **spare** *2 pl.pr.* 398.

**sparrede** *p.p.* shut up, hidden 238.

**sparthe** *n.* battle–axe 238.

**speche** *n.* speech, debate 325.

**spedfully** *adv.* successfully, effectively 224.

**spedles** *adj.* unprofitable 325.

**speken** *inf.* utter 325.

**spende** *inf.* spend 224.

**spere** *n.* spear 238.

**spyces** *n.pl.* spices 339.

**spyres** *n.pl.* seedlings 398.

**sprede*** *3 sg.pr.subj.* cover, spread lavishly 485.

**sprynge** *n.* sapling 398.

**sqwyeres** *n.pl.* squires 194.

**standes** *v.* stand, remain, exist; **standes** *3 sg.pr.* 228, 382; **stondes** *3 sg.pr.* 70; **stondeth** *3 sg.pr.* 101.

**stedis** *n.pl.* horses 209.

**stele** *n.* steel 113, 142; **stelen** *adj.* made of steel 252.

**steppede** *3 sg.pa.* walked 35.

**sterlynges** *n.pl.* silver pennies 252.

**stynt(e)** *inf.* cease 107, 195; **styntt** *3 sg.pr.subj.* 229.

**stirre** *inf.* move, approach 127.

**stones** *n.pl.* precious stones 343.

**stremys** *n.pl.* waters 42, 460.

**strete** *n.* street 480.

**stryffe** *n.* arguing, contention 265.

**strike** *inf.intr.* strike, attack 229; *trans.* strike (blows) *inf.* 127; *3 pl.pr.* 107, 195.

**stroye** *inf.* destroy, ruin 229, 243; **stroyeste** *vp 2 sg.pr.* consume 265.

**stroke** *n.* blow 107, 127, 195; **strokes** *pl.* 142.

**stuffed(e)** *p.p.* stuffed, crammed 252, crowded 168, armed, equipped 142.

**sturte** *n.* violent behaviour 265. [OE *strūt*]

**sum** *adj.* a certain, some 383.

**swannes** *n.pl.* swans 340, 379.

**sweped** *p.p.* swept 46.

**swerdes** *n.pl.* swords 320.

**swete** *adj.* sweet 353.

**sweuen** *n.* vision 46.

**swyngen** *inf.* ~ **togedirs** meet in battle 320.

**swythe** *adv.* soon 46, 320, quickly 121.

## T

**tayte** *adj.* merry 477. [ON *teitr*]

**take** *inf.* choose, take 352; **tast** *2 sg.pr.* 445;

**takes** *3 sg.* 122; **take\*** *2 sg.pr.subj.* 469; **take** *imper.sg.* 448; **takynge** *vbl.n.* capture 2.

**tale** *n.* story, narrative 31, 247; proverb, lesson 445.

**tartes** *n.pl.* pies 341.

**tasselde** *p.p.adj.* adorned with tassels 82.

**tauerne** *n.* inn, tavern 277, 477.

**teche** *imper.sg.* instruct, direct, show 288, 477, 489.

**teeles** *n.pl.* teals 352.

**tell(e)** *inf.* relate, recount, tell 17, 26, 31; **tellys** *3 sg.pr.* 181; **tolde** *3 sg.pa.* 293; *p.p.* 445.

**ten** *adj.* ten 341.

**tene** *inf.* annoy, anger 247; **tenys** *3 sg.pr.impers.* 341, **tenyth\*** 358.

**tent** *n.* heed, attention 445.

**thay, they, þay** *pers.pron. 3 pl.nom.* they 37, 39, 53; **thaym, þa(y)m** *acc., dat.* 97, 162, 172, **hem\*** 15n.; **thaire, thayre, þair(e)** *gen.* 19, 39, 52, **hire** 13; **þamselfe** *pron. 3 pl.refl.* themselves, 360.

**than, then(e), þan, þen** *adv.* then, afterwards 16, 45, 241; further 64; *conj. after cp.* than 28, 56, 272.

**thare** *3 sg.pr.* needs 201n. [OE *þurfan*]

**that, þat** *pron.* that, it 76, 167, 488.

**that, þat** *rel.pron.* who, which, whom, that 5, 19, 22; he who 147, those who 409, that which 260, 444.

**that, þat** *conj.* that 106, 126, 133; so that 9, 341, 478; **loke ... ~** make sure 467, **sythen þat** since 1, 427.

**the, þe** *def.art.* 2, 4, 10.

**thefe** *n.* scoundrel, villain 228, 242.

**then(e)** see **than**

**þeraftir** *adv.* accordingly, *or* afterwards 362.

**therby** *adv.* besides, next to 335.

**ther(e), þer** *adv.* there 124, 147, 251; *indef.* there 3, 64\*, 172; **there aboute** thereabouts 280; *rel.* where, wherever 35, 123, 312.

**thi** see **thou**

**thies** see **this**

**thikke** *adj.* dense, crowded 190; *adv.* tightly, densely 113.

**thynke** *v.*[1] presume, think, expect, intend, imagine, plan, recall, remember; *inf.* 128; **thynk** *1 sg.pr.* 499; **thynkes** *3 sg.pr.* 68, 229; **thynken** *2*

*pl.pr.* 401; *3 pl.pr.* 107, 153, 195; **thynke** *imper.sg.* 103; **thoghte** *1 sg.pa.* 84. [OE *þencan*]

**thynke(s)** *v.*[2] *3 sg.impers.* seems 99, 146, 453; **thoghte** *3 sg.pa.* 47, 93, 202. [OE *þyncan*]

**thirde** *adj.* third 156, 344.

**this, þis** *dem.adj.* this 7, 69, 90; **thies** *pl.* 25, 54, 123; *pron.sg.* 130, 325, 338, *pl.* 152, 159.

**þofe** *conj.* although, even though 470, **all þofe** 420.

**thoo, þo** *pron.pl.* those 224, 442.

**those** *adj.pl.* those 317.

**thou, þou** *pron. 2 sg.nom.* you 105, 207, 258, 264\*; **the, þe** *acc., dat.* 247, 279, 369, *refl.* 279, 467, 474; **thi, thy, þi** *gen.* 104, 246, 250; **thyn** (before *h* and vowels) 268, 278, 279; **thiseluen, þiseluen** *pron. 2 sg.* yourself 264, 374, 389.

**thre(e)** *adj.* three 80, 117, 144.

**threpen** *3 pl.pr.* quarrel, scold 37.

**throly** *adv.* vigorously 37.

**throstilles** *n.pl.* thrushes 37.

**thurgh, þurgh** *prep.* through 476, by means of 2, 25, 171, throughout 299.

**thus, þus** *adv.* in this way 259, 362.

**tyde** *n.* season, time 165.

**til(l)** *conj.* until 55, 196, 469; **tyll** *prep.* to 38.

**tille** *inf.* cultivate 288.

**tyme** *n.* season 396, time 439; **tymes** *pl.* reigns 3.

**tynen\*** *inf.* enclose, fence in 288.

**titmoyses** *n.pl.* titmice 352.

**to** *adv.* too 224, 372.

**to** *conj.* until 245, 470.

**to** *prep.* to 99, 100, 199; as far as 111, 411, for 148, 398, as 499; *with inf.* 8, 20, 52.

**tofore** *adv.* before 434.

**togedir(e), togedirs** *adv.* together 25, 37, 106.

**tong(e)** *n.* mouth, tongue 364; language 67.

**tonne-hede** *n.* the end of a wine-cask 277n.

**towne, townn** *n.* town 377, 489.

**tounen** *3 pl.pr.* resound 358.

**tounnes** *n.pl.* casks 189.

**tresone** *n.* treason 2.

**tretys** *n.* composition *incipit.*

**trynes** *3 sg.pr.* proceeds, goes, rides 122. [OSw. *trina*]

**trompers** *n.pl.* trumpeters 358.
**trotte** *n.* gait 122.
**trotte** *inf.* run 489.
**trouthe** *n.* pledge 307, 452.
**tuly** *adj.* rich, fine (of cloth) red in colour 82.
**tuttynge** *pr.ptc.* fluttering, flaring 82. [?OE *tutian* or *tȳtan*]
**twa, two** *adj.* two 78, 79, 126.
**twayne** *adj.* two 158, 456, 482.
**twelue** *adj. as sb.* twelve, a jury 313.
**twenty** *adj.* twenty 206.

## V = U

**vmbestounde** *adv.* at times 100.
**vmbygon(e)** *p.p.adj.* surrounded 62, 118.
**vmbtourne** *adv.* bordering, all around 412.
**vnder(e), vndir** *prep.* under, beneath 34, 89, 173; *adv.* beneath 80.
**vnthrifte** *n.* extravagance 267.
**vntill** *prep.* toward 58, 473*.
**vp** *adv.* up 38, 70, 210.
**vpbrayd** *inf.* censure 426.
**vpbrayde** *p.p.* unfurled 149; pulled up 208.
**vsage** *n.* custom, law 130.
**vttire** *adv.* away, farther 468.

## V

**vayne** *adj.* empty, meaningless 294.
**vaynes** *n.pl.* veins, (fig.) spirits 479.
**venyson** *n.* venison 334.
**vouchesafe** *1 pl.pr.* permit, allow 427.

## W

**waye** *n.* way, journey 104, 122, 460; **wayes** *pl.* 208.
**wayte** *inf.* wait 437, **waytten** observe, consider 257; **waytted** *1 sg.pa.* peered 85, ~ **one wyde** *3 sg.pa.* looked around 213; **wayte** *imper.sg.refl.* look, watch 475, attend carefully 496.
**wayttinge*** *vbl.n.* feasting, revelry 266n. [cf. ON *veita veizlu*, mod. Icel. *veitingar*]
**wakede** *p.p.* remained awake 248; **wakynge** *vbl.n.* revelry 266.
**wale** *adj.*[1] pleasant 34. [ON *val*]
**wale** *adj.*[2] short 396n., great, rapid 460n. [EFris *wale*]
**walke** *inf.* wander, travel 257; **walked** *p.p.* 136.

**walles** *n.pl.* walls, buildings 12, 301.
**walt** see **weldys**
**waltered** *p.p.* tossed, turned 248.
**wandrynge** *pr.p.* wandering 32.
**wanhope** *n.* despair 309, 373.
**wanne** see **wynn**
**warmen** *inf.* warm, toast 450.
**warre** *adj.* aware 85.
**wasschen** *inf.* wash, cleanse 268.
**waste** *n.* waste, consumption 253, 473.
**waste** *inf.* waste, consume 450; **wastes, wastis** *2 sg.pr.* 439, 495; **wastes** *3 sg.* spends 230; **wasted*** *p.p.* 408.
**wastour(e)** *n.* waster *incipit*, 242, 246, 263.
**wate** see **w(i)ete**
**watir** *n.* water 44.
**wawes** *n.pl.* waves 12.
**waxe** *inf.* become 373, **waxen** *3 pl.pr.* 12.
**we** *pron. 1 pl.* we 5, 205, 207; **vs** *acc.* 205, 206, 244; **oure** *gen.* 69, 124, 152.
**webbe** *n.* tapestry, web 64.
**wedde** *inf.* marry 15.
**weddis** *n.pl.* pledges, mortgages 284.
**wedir** *n.* weather 437.
**wedis** *n.pl.* clothes 426, **wedes*** 420.
**wedowe** *n.* widow 280.
**wee hee** *exclam.* whee 282.
**weghethe** *3 sg.pr.* weighs 162.
**welcomes** *imper.pl.intr.* welcome 212n.
**weldys** *3 sg.pr.* enjoys 236; **walt** *3 sg.pa.* ruled, had dominion 420.
**wele** *n.* wealth, possessions 236, 253, 268n.; welfare, enjoyment 283.
**wele** *adv.* well, much, very 28, 161, 205, heavily 162, properly 492; **better, bettir** *cp.* more, better 225, 247, 365; **beste** *sup.* 30, 125.
**wellande** *pr.p.adj.* boiling 262; simmering 351.
**wenche** *n.* girl 280, 414.
**wende** *1 sg.pr.* go 497; **wiendes** *3 sg.pr.* 226; **wend** *2 pl.pr.* come 198; **went** *1 sg.pa.* wandered 32, left, went away 84; **wentten** *3 pl.* journeyed, travelled 161; **wende** *imper.sg.* go 104, 460; **went** *p.p.* tossed, turned 248.
**wene** *1 sg.pr.* know 186.
**wepyn** *inf.* weep, lament 331.
**were** *3 pl.subj.pr.* hold, possess 442n. [OE *werian*]
**wery** *2 pl.pr.refl.* curse, blaspheme 437, *3 sg.pr.subj.* curse 285; **weryed** *p.p.adj.* 242.

**werke** *n.* work, poetic work 30, 216, 366; **werkes** *pl.* deeds 285.

**werlde, worlde** *n.* world 7, 47, 120.

**werped(e)** *p.p.* filled 250; **werped** *p.p.adj.* woven 64.

**wer(r)e** *n.* war 140, campaign 497.

**werse** *adj.cp. as obj.* worse 290.

**weste** *adj.* west 32.

**westren** *adj.* western 7.

**wete** see **w(i)ete**

**whalles** *n.gen.sg.* whale's 181.

**what(t)(e)** *pron.interrog.* what 253, 369, 425; *rel.* 218, 279, 352; **whate** *adj.* 47, **whatt** 192; **what** *interj.* 119n.

**when** *adv.* when 9, 29, 166, then 118; *conj.* when, whenever 155, 248, 283, ~ ... **then** 12, 227.

**where** *adv.* where 200, 453, 458, wherever 476.

**whete** *n.* wheat 380.

**whi, why** *adv.* why, for what reason 219, 233.

**while** *n.* while, time 27, 109, 437.

**while(s)** *conj.* while, as long as 7, 108, 110.

**whylome** *adv.* once, formerly 19.

**whit(t)e** *adj.* white 144, 156, 175.

**white-herede** *adj.* white-haired 150.

**who** *pron.indef.* whoever, who 30.

**whoso** *pron.* whoever, if anyone 17, 88, 181.

**wy** *n.* man 7, 56, 120, **wye\*** 201; **wyes** *pl.* 136, 140, 497.

**wyde** *adj.* large 250, open 475; *adv.* far and wide 136; **one** ~ around 213.

**wyd(e)whare** *adv.* far and wide 257, 326.

**w(i)ete** *inf.* know, learn 84, 216, 366; **wote** *1 sg.pr.* 161, 191, 368; **wate** *2 sg.pr.* 389; **wiete** *3 sg.pr.subj.* 200; **wiste** *1 sg.pa.* 47, *3 sg.* 120.

**wyfe** *n.* woman, wife 280; **wifes, wyles** *pl.* 395, 408.

**wightly** *adv.* promptly, boldly 104.

**wikked(e)** *adj.* sinful, wicked 242, 285.

**wild(e)** *adj.* turbulent 12, undomesticated 346, 385.

**wyles** *n.pl.* cunning, trickery 5.

**wilfully** *adv.* deliberately 408.

**will** *n.* will, desire 15; **willes** *pl.* commands 104, whims, desires 395.

**will** *1 sg.pr.* desire, wish 472; *2 sg.pr.* will 468, **wilt** 496, **wolle** (verb of motion understood) 277; **will** *3 sg.pr.* 17, 18, 30; **wilnes** 216, 366; **wil(l)** *3 pl.* 224, 360,

393; **woldest(e)** *2 sg.pa.subj.* 375, 442; **wolde** *3 sg.pa.subj.* 308.

**wyndowe** *n.* window 475.

**wyn(n)** *v.* win, acquire, gather, harvest; **wyn(n)** *inf.* 179, 274, 390; **wynn** *1 sg.pr.* 230; **wyn** *3 pl.pr.* 442; **wanne** *3 sg.pa.* persuaded 162; **wynnynge** *vbl.n.* profit 161.

**wyne** *n.* wine 189, 213, 283.

**wyng** *imper.sg.* hurry, fly 473n.

**wynges** *n.pl.* wings 92, 117.

**wynner(e)** *n.* winner *incipit*, 222, 246.

**wyntter** *n.* winter 275, **wynttres** *gen.sg.* 266; **wyntere, wyntter** *pl.* 206, 299.

**wirche** *inf.* compose 30; do 201; work, labour 287; **wroghte** *3 sg.pa.* composed 25; created 296; embroidered 414; *p.p.* uttered, expressed 22, *p.p.adj.* costumed 71; fashioned 117.

**wyre** *n.* thread 118.

**wyse** *n.* fashion, manner 75, 110.

**wyse** *adj.* wise 10, 22, 316, knowing 6.

**wisse** *inf.* devise 308; **wysses** *3 sg.pr.* directs 226.

**wiste** see **w(i)ete**

**with** *prep.* with, through 2, 5, 14.

**withinn** *adv.* within 2, inwardly 22, inside 85, in 144, on 157; *prep.* within 132, 357, in the space of 369.

**withowt(ten)** *prep.* without 24, 262, 346.

**witt** *n.* craft, guile, skill, knowledge 5, 25, 56.

**witterly, wittirly** *adv.* clearly, certainly 200, 389. [Scand; cf. MSw. *vitterliga*]

**wittnesse** *n.* witness 30; *as vb. 3 pl.pr.* 189.

**wodcokkes** *n.pl.* woodcocks 351.

**wodd(e), woodd** *n.* timber, wood 396, 450; forest 34, 385.

**wod(e)** *adj.* mad, crazed 373, 465.

**wodwales** *n.pl.* woodpeckers 351. [unkn. cf. MLG *wedewale*]

**wodwyse** *n.* wild man of the woods 71n.

**wolle** *n.* wool 189, 250.

**wondires** *3 sg.pr.impers.* it amazes 392, 424.

**wondres** *n.pl.* marvels 84.

**wonne** *inf.* dwell, remain 385, 472\*, **wonnes** *3 sg.pr.* lives 249, lingers 280.

**woo** *n.* misery 262.

**worde** *n.* speech 263, 457; **wordes** *pl.* words 6, 22, 25, words of introduction, courtship 282.

**worthe(n)** *inf.* be, become 130, 159, 253; **worthes** *2 sg.pr.* 300; **worthe** *3 sg.pr.subj.* 245, 477; **worthe vp** *imper.sg.* get up 282.

**worthiere** *adj.cp.* better 56; **worthiliche** *adj.* great 34.

**worttes** *n.pl.* herbs, vegetables 346.

**wote** see **wete**

**wounder** *n.* marvel 236n.

**wo(u)ndirs** *3 sg.pr.impers.* amazes 392, 424.

**wrake** *n.* mischief, harm 198.

**wrechede, wrechide** *adj.* contemptible 324, 326.

**wrethe** *inf.* make angry 465, *2 pl.pr.subj.* 395.

**wrethyn** *p.p.adj.* curled, twisted 71.

**wriche** *n.* wretch 309, 424.

**wryeth** *3 sg.pr.* conceals, obscures 6n.

**wroghte** see **wirche**

**wronge** *n.* injustice, fault 200, error 439.

**wrothe** *adj.* angry, displeased 201; *as n.* anger, resentment 57; **wroth(e)ly** *adv.* 324, 423.

# INDEX OF NAMES